Praise for *Wide Open Spaces*

"I could read what Jim Palmer writes all day. He's honest, funny, and his perspective really gives you something to chew on. When you open up *Wide Open Spaces*, it's like opening up a window on the first day of fall after a long hot summer and letting that breeze rush in. It's refreshing and invigorating, and oh so welcome."

—Ernie Johnson, Jr.,
sportscaster for TNT/TBS

"Jim knows the mess of the world. Jim knows the mess of the church. And he still has the audacity to believe that love wins. Here he has created a book of stories and reflections that cannot help but leave you feeling closer to God—with a smile that isn't just for Sunday mornings—and filled with the hope that another world is possible."

—Shane Claiborne
activist, author, recovering sinner (thesimpleway.org)

"Jim Palmer, the hall of fame pitcher, changed speeds on his fastball. But *this* Jim Palmer, the author, changed lives in our locker room. It has been an absolute pleasure to pass this book out to some of my teammates. As I read the pages of each chapter, I felt God moving me further away from religion and closer to experiencing His desired freedom in Christ. If you want to escape the popular Christian treadmill or common Churchianity, *Wide Open Spaces* and *Divine Nobodies* are must-reads!"

—Paul Byrd
pitcher, Cleveland Indians

"My favorite spiritual practice is underlining books. I stopped underlining Jim Palmer's newest book because I found myself underlining the whole thing. Few books in life have brought my soul more pleasure, or profit, than *Wide Open Spaces*."

—Leonard Sweet
...ersity, George Fox University, wikiletics.com

"To anyone who has ever gasped for air within the claustrophobic confines of religion, to anyone who has ever held up her dukes to God in a desperate plea for honest contact, Jim Palmer suggests, 'Let's take this outside.'

Wide Open Spaces is an invitation to freedom beyond the boundary lines of organized religion (which is more a mix of cultural bias and corporate structures than a celebration of the Truth that sets us free). This book is guaranteed to raise both your eyebrows and your hopes, to stretch your doctrine even as it stretches your faith. Every word rings true, even as it startles, with this bold—and biblically supported—proposal: when we fulfill our true calling to be 'little Christs,' we partner with God as he works his perfect will, joyfully growing the kingdom 'on earth as it is in heaven.'"

—Kristyn Komarnicki
editor, PRISM magazine, Evangelicals for Social Action

"No sooner does one come to the understanding of seeing the divine in others then Jim pops another at us—in the reality of Wide Open Spaces. I love the way Jim connects his story with the stories of others, and how God can move in us, around us, about us, and through us to see the work in the kingdom. Sometimes life can be hard, but seeing the hand of God is a powerful way of expressing our walk—Jim does just that in this book. I would recommend it to anyone seeking to know more, find more, live more, understand more, and journey more with the divine in us all. Get ready to be 'Unzipped' as you explore the reality of God in many ways."

—John O'Keefe
founder/designer, ginkworld.net
"proof evolution is in flux"

"As a dedicated Christian currently in search of a church, I found Wide Open Spaces hope-inspiring and instructive. Ever since I became a Christian I have struggled with the question of church: not just which local church to attend, an ongoing problem for my family, but what church really is, or should be. The response of the church—that is, of pastors and churchgoers in my acquaintance—has only contributed to my struggle. While many have allowed a distinction between "church" and "the church," most are leery of taking the discussion much further, and some even question whether those who don't attend church can really be Christians at all. According to Jim Palmer, though, church is not a building or a set of activities or a certain group of people who get together weekly to worship God. Rather, church is 'everywhere, all the time, with everybody.' What a refreshing message to those of us whose pursuit of God takes place in large part outside the context of the established church."

—Patty Kirk
writer in residence and associate professor of English, John Brown University; author of *Confessions of an Amateur Believer* and *Starting from Scratch: Memoirs of a Wandering Cook*

"*Wide Open Spaces* is an unabashed invitation to sail out of the shallows of stagnant, repetitive Sunday-only religion and to sail out into the adventure of a life lived alongside Jesus in the wild, open currents of everyday life. As Jim attests, the rewards far outweigh the risks!"

—Wayne Jacobsen
author of *He Loves Me: Learning to Live In the Father's Affection*

"From the first chapter, it's clear that Jim has written a brave book. He's articulated much of the discontent I have felt with the church in America, and he's done it not with cynicism (which would've been easy) but with a frank and gentle wisdom. I put the book down grateful for the reminder that being a Christian means vastly more than adhering to the paradigm."

—Andrew Peterson
singer/songwriter

"A radical and welcome book about how to be an authentic Christian in a post-Christian world. Jim Palmer's new words on church, faithfulness, and finding God in new places are a gift to us all."

—Greg Garrett
author of *Crossing Myself* and *The Gospel According to Hollywood*

"It is a rare achievement for any artist to follow their first work—one that remains as highly acclaimed as *Divine Nobodies*—with a follow-on work that is unequivocally better than the first. Jim Palmer has done it with *Wide Open Spaces*. The reading of *Wide Open Spaces* is not optional. It's mandatory if you are one who desires to know God and be love in our world today. This book is an epic contribution to the way ahead. The implications of *Wide Open Spaces* are clear for the spiritual sojourner and the possibilities for a way of life for those who deeply desire something more in how they experience God on a day-to-day basis."

—Richard Dahl
author, creator, and editor of www.theporpoisedivinglife.com

"*Wide Open Spaces* chronicles Jim Palmer's search for something other than cultural Christianity, and it seems that along the way he found it. Having just read the book, I now feel drawn to begin that same search myself."

—Charles J. Powell
producer of *Faith Café*, Inspiration Networks

"Thank goodness *Wide Open Spaces* is done! I thought Jim was going to pass out from the heat as he pecked away on his laptop in that ugly rocking recliner in his garage."

—Jim's next door neighbor

WIDE OPEN SPACES

JIM PALMER

THOMAS NELSON
Since 1798

NASHVILLE DALLAS MEXICO CITY RIO DE JANEIRO BEIJING

Published in Nashville, Tennessee by Thomas Nelson. Thomas Nelson is a trademark of Thomas Nelson, Inc.

Published in association with the literary agency of the Daniel Literary Group, 1701 Kingsbury Dr., Suite 100, Nashville, TN 37215, www.danielliterarygroup.com.

Thomas Nelson, Inc. titles may be purchased in bulk for educational, business, fund-raising, or sales promotional use. For information, please e-mail SpecialMarkets@ThomasNelson.com.

To protect the privacy of individuals, some names and details have been changed.

Library of Congress Cataloging-in-Publication Data

Palmer, Jim, 1964–
   Wide open spaces / by Jim Palmer.
       p. cm.
   Includes bibliographical references and index.
   ISBN 978-0-8499-1399-0 (trade paper)
   1. Palmer, Jim, 1964- 2. Christian biography. I. Title.
BR1725.P225A3 2007
248—dc22   2007020683

Printed in the United States of America
07 08 09 10 11 RRD 9 8 7 6 5 4 3 2 1

Wide Open Spaces is dedicated to the Hokie Nation,
and in loving memory of all those Hokies who moved on
sooner than we expected on April 16, 2007.

Contents

**One question can be more instructive
than a thousand answers.**

—Socrates

Introduction

Where's Stephen King
When You Need Him?

Some of the earliest reviewers of my book *Divine Nobodies* said I had a knack for storytelling. Sure, there were also those who said my writing was a train wreck, but who listens to them? Anyway, I had all the encouragement I needed to leave behind the simpleton world of nonfiction and launch my illustrious career as a fiction writer. Armed with *The Elements of Style* by Strunk and White, I was ready to join the ranks of Tom Wolfe and Anne Rice.

Things got off to a great start. The idea for the novel jelled quickly. I decided to title it *Unzipped*. The story was a thematic combination of the films *Crash* and *The Matrix*, with a bit of *The Lord of the Rings* sprinkled in for good measure. A tragic event would throw together an unlikely group of people. While each of them searches for God in his or her own way, the reader wonders who is truly getting closer to the truth and who is drifting further from it. That's the *Crash* part.

For the characters getting it, most of what they thought they knew about God proves false and they are awakened to a whole new dimension of spiritual reality, à la *The Matrix*. They soon discover they must free the others from the illusory world. Feeling woefully inadequate, a *Lord of the Rings*–type fellowship develops among them and they help one another embrace their newly uncovered identities in God. The only hope for those still trapped in the illusory world is to be awakened by love. The kingdom of God is about to unfold in powerful ways through the simple acts of belief and love by this improbable collection of nobodies.

Can you see how this would have been a best-selling novel of Stephen King proportions? Speaking of Stephen King, I also read his book on how to write great fiction, *On Writing: A Memoir of the Craft*.[1] Now I was more than ready to apply my creative genius. So I brewed a big pot of gourmet coffee (okay, so it was Kroger's generic) and descended into my special writing room (my dog Jack's time-out room) to tap into that endless flow of inspired creativity every great fiction writer has. Minutes passed . . . days passed . . . weeks passed . . . months passed . . .

Well, let's just say that what I produced could only be considered "fiction" by people who believe stick people are art. Jack seemed to like it, but I feared humans wouldn't. The dialogue between characters wasn't much more advanced than cave people:

---

1. Stephen King, *On Writing: A Memoir of the Craft* (New York: Simon & Schuster, 2000).

Bob said, "Me Bob. Nice to meet you. Who you?"
Mary replied, "Me Mary. Nice meet you, Bob. Me and
Bob save world."

I got desperate as more time passed. In his book on writing, Stephen King says he wrote most of *The Tommyknockers* and virtually all of *Cujo* while intoxicated. I went to my wife, Pam, and asked how she would feel if I took up drinking. She didn't care for the idea.

Oddly enough, a few things Stephen King said in *On Writing* influenced my change in direction. King admits for many years being ashamed of his writing. "I was ashamed. I have spent a good many years—too many, I think—being ashamed about what I write."[2] His words rang true with me, and I had to admit to myself that I wanted to write a novel because it symbolized some sort of step up in the writing world. Eventually I discovered God wants me to be free from the need to seek worth and identity in becoming the next F. Scott Fitzgerald. The truth of who I am in God—the real Jim Palmer—can't be diminished even if my attempts at writing fiction don't amount to much more than cavemen and stick people. Suddenly I felt free to write in my quirky, unconventional, and nonfiction way.

Another influential comment by Stephen King, which he made in passing with no further elaboration, was this: "And while I believe in God I have no use for organized religion."[3] This reminded me of the reader I am writing

---

2. Stephen King, *On Writing: A Memoir of the Craft* (New York: Simon & Schuster, 2000), 39.
3. Ibid., 52.

for—the person who desires to know God as a person, not a program.

It is no secret that God can be lost beneath the waving banner of religion. *Divine Nobodies* is my story of how this happened to me.[4] Sometimes you have to disentangle God from religion, even Christ from Christianity, to find the truth. With the help of some unsuspecting nobodies, I uncovered a new starting line with God. As I've put one foot in front of another, I've experienced God in ways that are deeply transforming.

This book is not meant to convince you of anything. Trust me, it's not from lack of desire. But I've crossed the line of realization that people have to discover truth for themselves. We can encourage one another along in the process, but we can't make other people embrace our truth as their own. People embrace truth when they're ready for it.

So each chapter in this book offers a little more of my story—what I'm discovering about God, life, and faith as I live into, stumble into, even trip over the answer. My greatest hope for you as a result of reading this book can be captured in one word—*love*. Amid the upcoming pages, may you "grasp how wide and long and high and deep is the love of Christ, and to know this love that surpasses knowledge—that you may be filled to the measure of all the fullness of God" (Ephesians 3:18–19).

Venturing into the wide open spaces of God these past few years has meant *freedom*! But there have also been times of wondering if perhaps I was going off the deep end, and more than a few occasions I found myself at odds with Christians.

I know this all might sound a little whacked out. That's

---

4. Jim Palmer, *Divine Nobodies* (Nashville: Thomas Nelson Publishers, 2006).

why I saved you from having to read it in the form of bad fiction. I figured I better stick to saying it as plainly as I know how. I'm discovering there is exponentially more to God and knowing him than my previous theology would allow. You're about to find out how.

So here we go.

Me Jim. This book. Turn page.

chapter one

My God Can Whup Your God!

Is God a Belief System?

There are certain memories that stick with you. Like the first time I was given smelling salts. I was lying flat on my back on the thirty-five-yard line of the Blacksburg High School football field. Carroll County had just kicked off the ball, which sailed high but wasn't making much forward progress down the field. In fact, a sickening feeling grew in my stomach as the football began angling toward *me*, the guy who normally blocks. I was looking up in the sky, the opposing team charging down the field, my arms stretched out wide to receive the ball, and . . . ⚡. The next thing I remember was being rudely jolted back into the land of the living.

These last few years, God has supplied a few jolts of his own to rouse me from my religious slumber. One of those jolts was Connie's July 13 blog post, only nineteen words long. Connie is one of my MySpace friends, and from time to time I read her blog. July 13 was one of those times. I clicked on her blog and read this:

> I Hate You.
> You Hate Me.
> We Hate Them.
> They Hate Us.
> What does it take to change this?

These words planted a seed within me that has continued to germinate. Religion teaches that God is synonymous with a specific belief system. Each system claims to have "right" beliefs about God, which are passionately held by its adherents—so much so that hate, bitter resentment, bloodshed, and even war can result from disagreement about God. A brief overview of world history shows that bad things happen when religious belief systems clash. This is what Connie was feeling. She had experienced religious hate in her own world, was fed up, and voiced it in nineteen sobering words.

But what if God isn't a belief system? What if God is bigger than self, bigger than family, bigger than tribe, bigger than nation, and even bigger than any set of doctrines we try to wrap around him? Whereas religion sometimes brings out the worst in people, could the vision of a bigger God cause us to place higher value on expanding our circles of care and compassion and working toward a more peaceful world?

One of the most freeing discoveries these past few years in my relationship with God (and it's still sinking in) is that God is not a belief system or a fixed set of theological propositions. On the one hand, it seems patently obvious that a list of claims about God can't actually be God himself. There isn't a lockbox at the center of the universe containing a divine computer program with doctrinal code. Hopefully we've all realized that *The Hitchhiker's Guide to the Galaxy* is fiction and that the number forty-two doesn't answer anything of ultimate significance. And yet for many years, my Christianity was basically a well-worked-out and defined set of propositions and practices in the name of God. I said Jesus Christ was my Savior, but in reality I treated my belief system as if it were my savior. It was my belief in the right suppositions about Christ that made me eternally saved.

When the basis for being a Christian is your specific set of beliefs about God, the most important thing is being right. If someone comes around with contrary ideas, the logical conclusion is . . . well, their ideas must be wrong. It doesn't take an MIT grad to figure out two people with divergent views of God can't both be right. Therein lies all religious conflict; there must be winners and losers. It's a zero-sum game. The "win-win" mentality just doesn't fly.

For many years, my sense of well-being, comfort, safety, security, identity, and superiority in the world was based largely on being right about God. I was eager to take on theological debates. After I received my masters of divinity degree, I was confident I was "right" about God. When threatened, my response was akin to the little boy yelling, "My daddy can whup your daddy!" I was happy to be counted among the few, the proud, the saved who could emphatically say, "My God can whup your God! My belief system wins over your belief system. My book is better than your book. I win, you lose. I'll pray for you."

But from time to time, interactions with some people

prompted me to notice the difference between upholding certain doctrinal beliefs *about* God versus actually experiencing God on a firsthand basis. Take Melanie, for instance. Melanie worked at a nearby Panera Bread, where I often went to drink coffee and work on my laptop. I was normally the first one there when the doors opened, which afforded some chitchat time with Melanie before the morning rush. When things slowed down, she'd be out wiping tables, and we'd pick up our conversation where it left off.

Melanie is one of those people who is good at planting an inspiring thought in your head. One early morning I came in still half asleep, and she said with an endearing smirk, "You better wake up. You might miss something." Once while toasting my bagel, she suddenly turned to me and asked, "Jim, why do you think people fear God?" Melanie enjoyed talking about God. Her face would light up as she described feeling God's love during her drive into work. I was convinced she must be smoking something. Melanie seemed to experience God everywhere and saw all of life from a spiritual perspective.

It was difficult to pin down the theological specifics of what Melanie believed about God, because she spoke of God like one would a neighbor or friend. It was maddening! I could never seem to find a natural opening to pop the question concerning her view of the Trinity. I, on the other hand, had my theological p's and q's all in good order, but I didn't seem to be tuned into God's frequency much of the time.

Unbeknownst to me at the time, God was using Melanie to prepare me for receiving a message that was going to be hard for me to swallow. In fact, I would have swiftly rejected this message had it arrived just four or five months earlier.

The message was from God, and I recorded it in my journal so I could remember the exchange:

GOD: *Jim, do you think knowing me is a matter of having correct theology?*

JIM: *As opposed to what, false theology!? Wrong beliefs aren't going to get me anywhere.*

GOD: *And where do you think your right beliefs are going to get you?*

JIM: *Well, if I believe the right things about you, then . . . well . . . I'll know who you really are . . . right?*

GOD: *Jim, do you know the sun radiates heat?*

JIM: *Of course.*

GOD: *How?*

JIM: *Because I've felt it.*

GOD: *Are you sure it's not because a science book told you the sun radiates heat?*

JIM: *Well, let's just say I didn't need the science book to know it.*

GOD: *Do you need a set of correct beliefs about me in order to know me?*

How dare God speak to me, a seminary graduate, questioning the value of my scholarly, airtight, bulletproof theology! I had spent four years and piled up a lot of school debt constructing that theology. Maybe God didn't appreciate just how brutal it was surviving Dr. Magary's Hebrew class!

God did seem to have a point, though. If God is real, I should be able to know and experience him directly, not just know *about* him through some set of theological propositions. If something is really true (or real), it can't just be true because the Bible says so. If there was no Bible to inform me that God is love, I could still experience God's love since his love is rooted in Truth. Truth is eternal. Therefore, Truth had to have existed long before the Bible was completed and put together into one document, which didn't take place until the third century.

This begs the question, what did people do before there was a Bible from which theological propositions could be formulated? Somehow God and humans made due without a well-defined belief system in place. How did that work? For instance, in the book of Genesis, a man named Enoch, only a few generations removed from Adam and Eve, is described as a man who "walked with God" (5:22).

Well, okay. Get ready. This is where things get interesting. *Maybe a well-defined set of truth propositions about God isn't necessary for knowing and experiencing God.*

Perhaps what's true of God has always been true and the Bible simply bears witness to it. After all, aren't the Scriptures written out of people's personal encounters with God? When Paul wrote, "The fruit of the Spirit is love, joy, peace, patience, kindness, goodness, faithfulness, gentleness and self-control," he was describing his experience of God (Galatians 5:22–23). But people walked in love, joy, and peace as a result of knowing God long before Paul penned the phrase "the fruit of the Spirit."

Maybe this was the difference between Melanie and me. Melanie was actually *experiencing* God as goodness—as love, as joy, as peace. Perhaps this is what God was telling me in our conversation about the sun. God doesn't want me to construct some sophisticated belief system about him. God wants me to experience the warmth of his love upon my face, to bask in his beauty and goodness, to rest in him and be at peace, and be an expression of all of these in the world.

You don't see Jesus rounding up his disciples for a class on Trinitarianism or sending them home to study hermeneutics. Essentially, Jesus taught that knowing God comes down to love. In fact, Jesus said you could summarize everything that's ever been said about what God desires in this way: "Love God and love people" (Matthew 22:37–39).

Hmm . . . do you think it's possible that God wants *love* to be our belief system? Religion seems to want us to focus on affirming a certain set of doctrines about God. But come to think of it, knowing the doctrine of the Trinity has not changed my life. I've known the Nicene Creed for many years and can recite it, but it hasn't turned me into the "new creation" Paul talked about (2 Corinthians 5:17). I have found these past few years that love is the only force that has transformed me. The stick (fear) and the carrot (reward) may alter my behavior or attitude, but love is the only force that transforms my being. If God is the ultimate power, then he must be love, perfect love.

God continuously prompts me to understand him in terms of love. I recently came across an interview *Newsweek* did with eighty-seven-year-old Billy Graham. Talking about his journey with God, Graham said, "As time went on, I began to realize the love of God for everybody, all over the world." Later he said, "I spend more time on the love of God than I used to."[5] At one point, the interviewer asked Billy Graham

---

5. Jon Meacham, "Pilgrim's Progress," *Newsweek* (14 August 2006), available at http://www.msnbc.msn.com/id/14204483/site/newsweek/page/0/, accessed 27 May 2007.

about the different religions in the world and the challenge of determining who's right and who's wrong about God. He responded, "I believe the love of God is absolute. He said he gave his Son for the whole world, and I think he loves everybody regardless of what label they have."[6]

My friend Jeffrey was recently in a conversation with a friend who is a self-proclaimed atheist. Jeffrey asked him why he believed as he did. In response, his friend began describing a jaded and harsh view of God and concluded emphatically, "I could never believe in a God like that."

This response led Jeffrey to ask another question, a bit stranger than his first. He asked his friend, "Do you believe in love?"

His friend responded, "Do I believe in love? Of course I believe in love! Everybody believes in love. There's nothing greater than love. You can never have enough love or give enough love. My life and this world would be so much better off if there was more love."

So Jeffrey asked, "What would you say if I told you God *is* love?" After pondering it for a moment, his friend replied in astonishment, "Well, if you're telling me God *is* love, then I'm no longer an atheist."

There are an endless number of things that divide people in our world. I'm becoming increasingly convinced God shouldn't be one of them. When the Scriptures say, "God is love" (1 John 4:8), maybe God was offering a center large enough for all people to seek truth peacefully. Religion, par-

---

6. Jon Meacham, "Pilgrim's Progress," *Newsweek* (14 August 2006), available at http://www.msnbc.msn.com/id/14204483/site/newsweek/page/0/, accessed 27 May 2007.

ticularly religious leaders, stirs up debate about whether Jesus is God. Something about this debate seems insane. Setting religion aside for a moment, who in their right mind wouldn't want Jesus to be God? I'm not sure I could construct a better God with my wildest imagination.

If someone came up to me and asked, "Jim, are you interested in knowing God? Before you answer, let me tell you about him. He always loves and accepts you without condition. His motive in all things is love, and he always has your best interests in mind. He desires your freedom and wants to be your source of love, truth, peace, joy, and goodness. He is full of compassion and understands the pain and suffering of the human journey from personal experience. Knowing him heals your deepest wounds and extinguishes your worst fears. His main principle for life is to love. Are you interested?" my answer would be, "Duh!"

During Jesus Christ's life on earth, he gathered a small group of people who devoted their lives to knowing and interacting with him. Knowing Christ helped them see and live in the world in a different way. They became more like Christ as they hung out with him. Many called these folks "disciples," or apprentices, of Christ. They learned things like: love God, others, even your enemies; let he who has not sinned cast the first stone; put the needs of others above your own; care for the poor and marginalized. In time, this group became so much like Christ himself, people referred to them as "little Christs."[7]

---

7. See Acts 11:26. Some evidence suggests the term was first used in a negative sense. Imagine a bratty kid pointing his finger and yelling, "Copycat, copycat!" Either way, the point is that these disciples were seen as clones of Christ.

Eventually this term was slightly modified into "Christian" and later became the label for an entire belief system named "Christianity." The "Christian" label spawned efforts to add increasing definition to its meaning. Once you've labeled and defined something, you've established what it is and isn't, who's in and who's out. In this case, being "in" was a matter of having certain beliefs about God. I once assumed that the earliest Christians (as well as most Christians down through history) more or less all agreed to the same doctrines about God and Jesus. It was quite a shock to discover this isn't true. In fact, the differences of opinion among Christians motivated people in positions of ecclesiastical power to create creeds as a litmus test for authenticating yourself as a Christian.

I'm thinking maybe this all was a big mistake.

What the term *Christian* originally referred to has been replaced by the idea of affirming certain beliefs about God. In fact, for most of my life, I believed that agreeing to four or five theological statements about God and Jesus Christ made me decidedly Christian. This seemed pretty harmless. God is infinite and the Bible contains sixty-six books, so it was comforting to know that the really important stuff was condensed into a statement of faith that fit nicely on the back panel of my church brochure.

On one occasion the disciples declared that if Jesus would "show them the Father," their lives would be forever changed. Jesus essentially replied, "Look no further. The heart and nature of God is right now on display before your eyes— *me*" (John 14:8–9).

Jesus didn't come to start a new religion; he came to reveal God. Why? Because God knew if humankind could physically experience who he is, we would want to know him, and knowing him would change us. It worked! The love of God on display in Jesus attracted people like a magnet. Hanging out with Jesus began transforming people's hearts, way of life, and relationships with others. Jesus was so compelling that people left everything to follow him.

That is, everyone except the religious establishment. The idea that God could be known simply through interacting with Jesus was threatening. Heck, if you could experience God directly, why would you need them and their elaborate system of religious rules and rituals? Maybe God wasn't so complex and hard to know after all. Maybe it just came down to . . . well . . . Jesus.

In the apostle Paul's mind, this truth transforms lives and changes the world. He wrote, "And this is the secret: Christ lives in you" (Colossians 1:27 NLT). We come to know God as we interact with Christ within us. God is not a belief system of truth propositions; he is a living spiritual reality within us. Two thousand years later, this is still the secret to knowing God.

As it was when God spoke to me that day, I realize the idea of this chapter could be hard for the typical Christian to swallow. Part of me felt I should add a bunch of caveats saying how important it is we actually do have our facts right about God. However, if we have relationship with God and are interacting with the living Christ within, doesn't it stand to reason that God will lead and guide us accordingly? Would God lead us into falsehood and lies? Didn't Jesus say his Spirit within us would guide us in all truth?

So the other day I went back to Panera Bread. Melanie wasn't working on that particular day, but I got to thinking about her. God uses Melanie and others like her to prompt me to see for myself that God is bigger (and better) than my best conceived notions about him. On the back of a napkin, I scribbled out the truth I know of God through experiencing Christ within me. This is what I wrote:

God is unconditional acceptance.
God is perfect peace.
God is total freedom.
God is unreserved joy.
God is continuous life.
God is gentle compassion.
God is unwavering goodness.
God is unbroken favor.
God is kindhearted forgiveness.
God is breathtaking beauty.
God is absolute truth.
God is love.

Maybe that is my statement of faith. This God seems bigger than any belief system religion can produce.

chapter two

Humankind Is from Mars, God Is from Venus

Can What We're Feeling Inside Be God?

One afternoon a friend and I were in downtown Nashville to see a Tennessee Titans football game. We parked the car and walked over to 2nd Avenue to grab a bite to eat before kick-off. The atmosphere was electric, and the streets and restaurants were bustling with people. We finally got a seat at Demos', which was jam-packed. While waiting for our food, I was suddenly overwhelmed with the realization that I loved all these people . . . even the Jacksonville Jaguar fans. Other than my friend Doug, all the people in the restaurant were total strangers, yet I felt we belonged to each other as one family and we could not be unlike one another. I felt this exhilarating joy of being human, a member of the race in which God himself came and lived. The sufferings and failings of the human condition seemed powerless compared to the truth of what we all are. If only all these people could understand this! But how do you explain it? How do you tell people they are walking around as reflections of God's perfect love?

This was but one of many "inner episodes" that began happening more frequently as I continued down the road of knowing God beyond religion. There was no rhyme or reason to when or where these episodes occurred—pushing a cart through the grocery store, watching my daughter's soccer practice, driving in the car, walking my dog Jack in the woods.[8] Without warning, a moment of bliss enveloped my entire being like walking out of a stuffy room into a beautiful, seventy-five-degree day. Unconditional love, complete freedom, perfect peace, and joy radiated from the center of my being to the surface of my skin.

When I experienced these deep feelings, I'd start looking around expecting to lock eyes with someone else who felt it as well. At times I wondered about my sanity—it doesn't take much to make me wonder. I can only compare it to how I felt when I was in the hospital, hooked up to an IV morphine drip. My wife, Pam, said a slap-happy grin took over my face right before I mumbled something about being the happiest man on earth and how the Braves were going to win the World Series. I could envision some guru sitting atop a mountain in deep meditation experiencing this sort of spiritual high, but me standing in a Saturday-morning line at Home Depot?

No matter how much I tried passing off these experiences as flighty, TGIF kinds of feelings, or attributing them to something outside myself like a stunning sunrise or beau-

---

8. Several things have changed since the writing of *Divine Nobodies*. We had to put our cat Daisy to sleep due to kidney disease, but we adopted Jack from the local animal shelter. Some things haven't changed: we still have that lame fifteen-inch television with foil-wrapped rabbit ears.

tiful melody, I knew there was more to it than that. Circumstances or people may have stimulated it, but this was most definitely something welling up from deep inside me. It wasn't contingent upon any particular external happenings; it just as easily happened on a rainy Monday or while I was under the sink trying to "repair" our garbage disposal.[9]

It was baffling. What was causing this? There was no logical explanation. I was not on drugs, I had not yet heard of *The Secret*, and I could only remember having watched *Oprah* once in my entire life.

I was hesitant to attribute these experiences to God because they felt too much like . . . uh . . . feelings. This was problematic because my religious conditioning taught me to mistrust my emotions. Following your feelings was akin to trusting a three-year-old with a loaded gun. We know that people who act on their feelings end up doing terrible or crazy things, like having an extramarital affair, going in debt for a Harley Davidson, or calling in sick in order to lie around and watch daytime television while eating Ben & Jerry's ice cream all day long. Yes, it's true, the first thing the Bible says about humankind is how we are all made in God's image, but it's foolish to think this trickled on past our brains all the way down into the dark well of our "sinful" emotions. The God's image thing simply didn't get that far. The important part is your head, where right beliefs, rational thinking, and objective, logical processes flow.

So I decided to try a little experiment. Whenever these

---

9. Pam made me put this in quotes because I didn't connect all the PVC pipes back together quite right, and there are leaks. In her mind, putting three of her Tupperware containers under the sink in various places to catch drips doesn't qualify as a true repair.

moments happened, I intended to stop and allow myself to soak it all in and then go with whatever these feelings seemed to be telling me. I'd have to say this decision is a little out of character, as I tend to be a self-doubting person. If I had to choose between Robert Frost's "two roads diverged in a yellow wood," I'd quickly be off on the well-traveled one. I may have never started down the untried road if I hadn't felt secure in God's unconditional love and acceptance. Fear of God's disapproval and punishment had always kept me well within the lines drawn by religious tradition. But now God's grace empowered me to explore beyond the borders, putting one foot in front of the other into the wide open spaces of his love.

I wasn't ruling out a loss of sanity just yet, but I knew God loved me, crazy or not, and would let me travel only so far down my "road less traveled by" if it wasn't really leading anywhere worthwhile.

My little experiment produced some alarming results. Surprisingly, my feelings did not tell me to become a polygamist, go on a shopping spree at Best Buy, or become a New York Yankees fan. Instead, whenever I homed in on these feelings, they primarily altered the way I viewed other people. I began recognizing and affirming God's image within everyone. It was like I could see something deeper in people than what showed up as their exterior behavior and attitudes.

To the guy ahead of me in line, the cashier may have been nothing more than a disheveled, overweight, ill-tempered woman who TiVo's *General Hospital* and has questionable taste in eye shadow. To me, I looked past her frayed appearance and harsh demeanor and saw that she was never going to be any more perfect than she already was. She was created in the image of God, who is perfect love and absolute goodness;

whatever imperfections she displayed had been forgiven in Christ and she was now the apple of God's eye. So as I stood before her at the register, that's the person I related to, not the disheveled and ill-tempered one.

I wondered if this could be the root of humankind's demise. Perhaps, people such as the cashier were not seeing themselves as God did. She was like the guy who is starving because the rocky and irregular surface of his land won't produce a crop, but unknown to him a huge vein of gold exists deep beneath the surface. How was I going to wake people up to the truth? I wanted to stand atop a table at IHOP and announce to everyone they weren't the worthless losers they thought they were. I imagined pulling up to a traffic light beside a Harley Fat Boy with some gnarly look-ing dude in a leather vest sporting twenty-inch biceps and a demon tattoo. How would he respond if I rolled down my window and said, "Excuse me, sir. Do you realize you are a living expression of perfect love?"

So I started reasoning through all this. *Okay, I'm having these experiences of deep feelings of love, joy, and peace radiating within me. When I listen to these feelings, they tell me to affirm God's image in everybody.* I guess that should have been enough to convince me I was experiencing God. However, it wasn't until I came across a little story in the Bible that I was convinced of the divine source of my deep feelings. The story from the Gospel of Luke is about two men who were traveling on foot to the village of Emmaus.

Following Jesus' crucifixion, two heartbroken men are walking along a road, sharing their bewilderment and despair over Jesus' death. Suddenly a stranger joins them. Luke tells the reader this stranger is Jesus, but the two men do not recognize him. Well, actually, as we discover by reading on, this isn't entirely true. The men actually did experience Christ on a spiritual level. According to the story, eventually they realize this stranger is in fact Jesus. Putting two and two together, one of them says, "Were not our hearts burning within us while he talked to us on the road?" (Luke 24:32).

What were they referring to when they described this experience of their "hearts burning"? Was it heartburn from one too many matzo balls? I don't think so. Even though they were not consciously aware of it, they experienced Christ deep within their hearts. Admittedly, *feelings* might not be the best word to describe this reality, but I haven't found any better word. It's simply something you feel.

Perhaps the most significant thing about the story is how it ends. The stranger agrees to have dinner with the two men. During dinner, Jesus opens their eyes in order to recognize him. Once they do, Jesus mysteriously vanishes. Why? Because Jesus was teaching them it was time to begin interacting with him on a spiritual level, not a physical one. The two men had been despairing over Jesus' crucifixion, but Jesus knew his death was necessary. Until they let go of the physical Jesus of Nazareth, they could not walk in the spiritual reality of Christ living within them. This is borne out in the remainder of the New Testament through words such as Paul's in 1 Corinthians 15:45: "The Scriptures tell us, 'The first man, Adam, became a living person.' But the last Adam— that is, Christ—is *a life-giving Spirit*" (NLT, emphasis added). Notice that Paul refers to Christ as a "life-giving spirit."

Most of my Christian life I had been fixated on the physical Jesus of Nazareth. Bible-story picture books show Jesus as a suave and caring bearded man in robe and sandals. Mel

Gibson's film *The Passion of the Christ* depicts a more life-like Jesus as a first-century Jew. The Catholic crucifix shows Christ's body on the cross. Jesus' youth is imagined in the novel *Christ the Lord* by best-selling author Anne Rice. Museums are filled with art depicting the image of Jesus and the events of his life. You can even get the image of Jesus on your pancakes. I recently discovered the JesusPan, a cooking pan made of durable steel and topped with a nonstick coating. The advertisement reads, "Put the image of Jesus RIGHT ON FOOD! Worship at every meal with JesusPan. Imagine serving Heavenly Hotcakes at the next church breakfast."[10]

My own imagination puts Jesus on a throne in heaven next to the Father, one day returning in the clouds, perhaps upon a horse, still wearing a robe and sandals. But how can this be right if Jesus himself said he lives within us? Does this mean if I cut you open I will find a bearded Jewish man inside you? No, Paul said Christ is a "life-giving spirit." Too often Christianity is a religion built around the historical figure Jesus of Nazareth, rather than a spiritual reality emanating from Christ the "life-giving spirit" within.

If Christ is a life-giving spirit, then what "life" is he "giving"? The answer has to be, the *life of God*. What is the life of God? Jesus of Nazareth demonstrated it. Virtually all people recognize that Jesus lived a life of perfect love.

What is love? Is it a thing? Can you hold it in your hands? No, it's something spiritual; you feel it deep within you and it takes shape in your thoughts, words, and actions. Have

---

10. Right now on jesuspan.com you can get two pans for $29.99! It's hard to pass up this deal. Unfortunately, I've had my eye on those "Got Jesus?" baseball hats. Maybe I'll get the hat and see if the JesusPan comes down to three pans for $29.99.

you ever felt love? Have you ever expressed love? Has it ever dawned on you that when you did, you were experiencing the life of God within you and through you? Our experience of love is the by-product of the spiritual presence of Christ within us. Apart from Christ and the life of God he supplies, love would not be possible. Jesus did not just *do* loving things; his state of being was and is love.

I see now that "accepting Christ" involves receiving and living my identity in Christ as love. Step one is simply realizing that when you experience love as an in-feeling or over-flowing expression, you are experiencing the reality of Christ.

You've never seen the wind, but you have felt the effects of the wind such as a cool breeze across your face on a hot summer day. Paul says the "fruit" (or effects) of Christ within are things such as love, joy, peace, and goodness. Jesus referred to it as abundant life (John 10:10). How do you experience these spiritual qualities? It's something you feel.

Didn't Jesus say there is nothing good but God? (Mark 10:18; Luke 18:19). So anytime I experience something good, I'm experiencing God. Have you ever been looking at your spouse or child and felt such strong feelings of love wash over you? Or followed a soaring hawk through the deep blue sky and suddenly felt perfectly at peace? Have you ever encountered someone in emotional pain, and an overwhelming surge of compassion made you want to throw your arms around him and tell him you loved him? Or hiked out to an overlook and felt immense joy as you surveyed a breath-taking canyon? In each of those moments you were experiencing God.

Maybe you've been experiencing God your entire life but missed it because you weren't aware that God expresses himself inside of you through feelings. Apparently humankind is from Mars, and God is from Venus. We want to figure God out in our head, while God wants us to feel him in our heart.

The Bible, especially Jesus himself, says all sorts of things that seem a little crazy, perhaps even heretical, if you take them seriously and flesh out the implications. Even with a divinity degree under my belt, I still wonder why people fiercely defend the literal translation of the Bible when it comes to historical facts and details but do not exert the same passion and energy proclaiming its spiritual truths. If God created me as a being with emotions, it only stands to reason that my emotive capacity is an aspect of who God is and therefore a significant way God expresses himself in and through me. You don't have to be an academic scholar in order to know God; you only have to be capable of having feelings. Authentic Christianity is still the best-kept secret. Its claims are not tried and found wanting, but found too simple and made more complicated accordingly.

I'm discovering that a significant element of living the Christian life is following my feelings. By saying that, I'm assuming you understand that acting on lust, pride, selfishness, hate, and greed is not what I'm talking about. We have no evidence in Christ that God is any of those things, and so obviously if you are experiencing them, you can't be experiencing God. What I'm finding instead is that when I follow those deep, "burning heart" kinds of feelings, I live as Christ. Let me give you an example.

I was on my way to California to speak at a conference. I arrived at the airport with plenty of time to spare and struck up a conversation with a man who was waiting for the same flight. We seemed to hit it off, and I was enjoying our chat.

It didn't take long for me to pick up on the fact that he was a wounded and dispirited sort of soul. He was a pharmaceutical rep on his way to a training conference that he dreaded attending. His passion was photography; he had twice tried opening his own photography studio and failed miserably. He even turned his laptop around and showed me several of his photos.

As our conversation went on, he was not reluctant to share more personal details about the last few years of his life. Right in the middle of his recounting a litany of failed relationships, I suddenly felt within me a surge of God's compassion and love for him. What I did next shocked me. Despite not being a touchy-feely guy, I reached over and firmly placed my hand atop his shoulder. I looked him squarely in the eye and spoke directly to him from those deep feelings. I told him that God did not look upon him as a failure and that the photographs he had shown me were beautiful to God.

The instant it all finished coming out of my mouth, I thought, *Oh my gosh, what in the crap did I just say?!* The next thing I heard was, "How do you know?"

It gets worse. As confident as Peyton Manning on a Sunday afternoon, I answered, "Because I just now felt inside me God's love for you."

He just stared at me for a few moments with an amazed look on his face. Finally he replied, "No one has ever said anything like that to me before."

Something beyond words happened in that short exchange. We both experienced it, and it was transformational. This is where I learned that when I allow those feelings of God within me to be expressed in some way such as in words or actions, the power of God is released into the world and anything can happen.

Our seven-year-old daughter, Jessica, launched her acting career last Friday night. She was in a play entitled *In the Halls of the Snow Queen*. Okay, so she wasn't the Snow Queen. Instead Jessica was playing two parts, a tree and a street urchin. Snow Queen, Schmo Queen—everyone knows a play stands or falls with the tree! Sure, you might not recognize it at first, but you'd be the first one complaining at any play where the tree didn't carry its weight. The creative interpretation of a tree is critical. Since the beginning of time, seven-year-old girls have stood on stages and offered their theatrical rendering of trees. Only a few succeed. I'll guarantee you, Wynona Rider once stared into an audience while struggling to keep her arms held high as a tree.

So Jessica's scene finally comes. Suddenly the most beautiful tree in the entire world appears on stage right before my eyes. A smile is beaming from her face and her arms are stretched high. I am seized by overwhelming feelings of love for her. In that moment, I feel I would sacrifice everything in the world for my Jessica. But then those feelings of love give way to a deep and hurting sadness. I cannot remember ever having felt being so intensely loved as a little boy by my own dad. So there I sit amid the crowd honed in on Jessica, feeling love and sadness. And God reminds me of something: we are sharing these feelings together. I was experiencing God's love for Jessica as my own feelings, and I was experiencing God's sadness for what I didn't receive as a little boy. In my love and in my sadness, I was experiencing God.

For years I was taught that "faith" is believing there is a God even if you can't experience him. Maybe instead, faith is believing that what you are experiencing *is* God.

chapter three

Here Is the Church,
and Here Is the Steeple . . .

Can Church Be Everywhere, All the Time, with Everybody?

Our lives are filled with choices, but sometimes others read too much into them or make assumptions that aren't necessarily true. For instance, we homeschool our daughter Jessica, but it's not because we think public schools are evil. We have friends who are public-school teachers, and some of Jessie's favorite playmates attend public schools. Pam and I don't drink alcohol, but it's not because we think drinking alcohol is a sin. A person can choose to abuse alcohol, or a person can choose to drink alcohol responsibly. Our reasons for not drinking alcohol are practical, not theological. I have a PC and not a Mac. It's not because I'm a "PC guy." I have a PC because it was the most inexpensive option I could find at the time, and cost was my primary concern. When it's time to get another computer, who knows, I may very well get a Mac.

In this chapter, I'm going to be describing what "church"

is for me these days. It's possible what I describe is unlike anything you've experienced or would even consider to be church as you have known it. However, it would not be correct to assume that I think my way of being the church is the "right" way and that others should adopt it. My journey has involved leaving organized church. Even as God led me *away* from organized church, I'm sure God also leads people *to* organized church for various reasons. Throughout my lifetime, I have encountered many different types of churches— liturgical church, traditional church, contemporary church, seeker church, purpose-driven church, home church, and emergent church. Each of these expressions of church has unique elements that I found meaningful in some way to my relationship with God.

Though I've experienced many different forms of church, there have also been some common elements that have been true of all of them. These include:

- An organizational identity with a name and 501c3 legal status
- A specific location(s) identified as the primary place or central hub where church happens (such as a church building, community center, school, or someone's home)

- Professional clergy or paid staff presiding over and managing the major affairs of the church
- Some configuration of public worship services, programs, groups, classes, meetings, events, and committees as the primary means for facilitating worship, fellowship, discipleship, service, benevolence, and mission

In fact, for seven years I served as the senior pastor of a church that had all the above elements. In our church, we experienced God powerfully at work in and through our lives in all sorts of awesome ways. To be fair, however, there were also things I did and encouraged that put up barriers to people knowing God. Our church simultaneously functioned on three levels:

- A *cause*—expressing the love of Christ to the world in word and deed
- A *community*—a fellowship of people encouraging and supporting one another
- A *corporation*—an organization with bills to pay, budgets to balance, buildings to maintain, programs to operate, and paid personnel

Most people would agree that the *cause* and *community* aspects of church are the most important, while the *corporate* side is a matter of practical necessity and efficiency. Yet the part I increasingly focused on was the *corporate* side. There were two reasons for this that stand out, neither of which I'm particularly proud.

First, too much of my personal identity was wrapped up in leading a "successful" church, which was measured in terms of size (attendance, budget, and buildings). The bigger the better! As senior pastor, my value and necessity in the system was based on my seminary degree and my position as the top person in the organizational hierarchy to lead and grow the church. There was plenty of reinforcement to stay focused on numbers. At every denominational or church leadership conference I attended, the questions were always of the "How many . . . ?" sort—how many people attending services, enrolled in Sunday school, participating in small groups; how many staff, dollars, and square feet of building space. The conference speakers, those held up as examples of success, always seemed to be pastors of megachurches.

Another reason I focused on the corporate side of church life was because of this idea I had that people needed such a system in order to grow spiritually and function together as a community and a cause. That's the nice way of putting it. The not-so-nice assumption was that if people were left to themselves to function without such a system and outside the watchful eye of trained pastors and staff leaders, they would digress spiritually, we would all risk falling into theological heresies, and everything would unravel into chaos.

I mentioned that my focus on the corporate side of church created certain barriers for people to know God. It should be of no surprise that if your personal identity, the expectations of others, and the means through which you generate a living wage all rest upon growing and sustaining a church as an organizational entity, then you are going to especially emphasize to people the need to participate in and support the system. I came dangerously close to implying that organizational involvement was the very essence of Christianity. A Christian faithfully attended services, programs, events, and classes, tithed, filled a needed position or served on a committee in the church, and pulled his or her weight in contributing to a steady stream of visitors.

Looking back, I sometimes wonder if we really were a "community." Seems like what we were facilitating was mostly meeting-based relationships. People would attend services, classes, programs, and groups, but outside the scheduled meeting time, there wasn't much interaction between these people the rest of the week until the next meeting rolled around. When the class or group came to an end, for all practical purposes so did the "relationships."

Here are some other ways I hindered people's relationship with God by focusing on the church as an organization. As you read these, keep in mind that regardless of what you tell people in sermons, the medium *is* the message that folks are going to pick up on.

First, even though we all know church is people, verbally and nonverbally I implied that church is a place, location, and building, and happens on certain days and times during the week. In many cases, this emphasis defined Christian living almost solely in terms of organizational involvement. "Worship" was something that happened on Sunday mornings, and "outreach" was a program you signed up for in the lobby.

Second, despite the fact that the Scriptures teach that all believers are equally equipped with the necessary spiritual resources for knowing God and ministering to others, our organizational hierarchy of pastors and staff encouraged an unhealthy dependency by the congregation upon these few. Staff personnel were viewed as individuals with a closer relationship with God and with greater biblical knowledge and spiritual wisdom. Parents relied on the children's ministry program and staff for the spiritual formation of their children. So the kids were naturally learning that other people, who know more than Mom and Dad, were responsible to teach them about God.

Third, though Jesus emphasized that people change from the inside out, our church often focused on external things as measurements of Christian maturity. The people who dressed nicer, attended more services and activities, prayed out loud in front of others, gave the most money, quoted Scripture, were up on stage, held more jobs in the church, invited the most visitors, had well-behaved children, and had no bad habits were considered more spiritual than people with less of the above.

 Fourth, as a church we also separated the giver (tithing or otherwise) from the actual recipient of the gift by employing an Old Testament system of giving. For example, we would quote Malachi 3:10: "bring the whole tithe into the storehouse," which we defined as the church organization. This process implied to the receiver that the church (as an organization) knows better to do with your tithe or gift than you do. We never actually said this out loud, but the process sent this message. The method also complicated the process of getting the gift to the person in need. The giver and receiver were not able to either express the reason they gave or their thanks for receiving the gift, both of which God uses as part of the process of transforming both the giver and receiver. Giving to whom God directs, when God directs, was less likely since people were conditioned to think of giving as an act of organizational involvement.

It seems so odd to me now that I ever thought of "church" as a place, program, or organization. This amazes me, given my roughly twenty-five years of deep involvement within this configuration of church. After leaving professional Christian ministry, my continued growth in God sparked a revolution of identity. My biological identity says I am the son of human parents and the sum total of a lot of hurt and heartache. My occupational identity was a religious leader striving to achieve and maintain guru status in the eyes of people. Then I discovered my spiritual identity, a living manifestation of God who exists to know God and express God and his kingdom. Accepting my spiritual identity freed me to *be* the church beyond the system I previously depended upon for worth and significance. My values changed. For the first time in my life, I realized the significance of a handful of significant and growing relationships.

The last few years I've discovered it's not necessary to have buildings and classrooms, staff and programs, or even incorporate as a 501c3 organization and have a name in order to be the church. You can if you want to, but you don't *have* to. Regardless of how you do it, what constitutes church is *relationships*—with God, people, and the world. For me, "church" is taking place in some form or fashion everywhere, all the time, with everybody. It involves an endless number of interactions and encounters that largely go unnoticed by the rest of the world. But it's through these very unassuming daily happenings that God is transforming others and me.

When I say our experience of church is "everywhere, all the time, with everybody," what I mean is that we experience the significant components typically associated with church life—such as worship, discipleship, fellowship, mission, service, accountability, and giving—through an infinite number of combinations of places, times, and people. For the most part, these combinations are not predetermined or scheduled in advance. This way of church depends on two things: (1) being consciously aware of who and what is happening around me as daily life unfolds, and (2) being intentional about discerning and acting upon the opportunities everyday living, interactions, and relationships offer. Here are some examples:

- A friend e-mails me to see if I want to have coffee on Saturday morning at the Billy Goat Café. He and I always have plenty to share in terms of what we are experiencing with God. When we get together, it's an iron-sharpening-iron time that fuels our desire to know God.

- On Tuesday afternoon at the post office, I get into a conversation with the guy behind me as we wait in a long line. He points to my Virginia Tech baseball hat and tells me his daughter just started college there. He's a veterinarian. We recently got a dog and had not yet decided upon a vet. Perhaps God is trying to place him and me in each other's lives.

- Sunday morning we are hiking at Radnor Lake with some friends. During one part of the hike, the sun's rays suddenly break through the tall trees, causing everything to glisten. Everyone stops. We stand in wonder and marvel at the beauty, and our hearts are turned toward God in worship.

That's not to say we don't ever plan something in advance. Most Wednesday evenings, a group of us meets at Starbucks for conversation. Every Monday night, some friends invite all their neighbors over for dinner. Everyone on Saint Charles Court knows Monday is spaghetti night at the Harris home. On Sunday mornings, except in the summer, Pam and Jessica are involved in the Good Shepherd children's program at an Episcopal church across town. Occasionally we attend a worship service or some event at other local churches in our community. For a time, a group of families met in a home to take Communion together. Right now we are in a season where we choose to celebrate Communion at home as a family. Another church in our community offers a monthly Taizé service, which I sometimes attend and always enjoy.

In the midst of all this diversity, I connect with a solid social network of people that keeps growing. It's a diverse network of folks involved in one another's lives. We love one another, serve one another, teach and encourage one another, give our financial and material resources to one another as there is need, and bear one another's burdens. We do life together.

It's been quite a ride getting to where we now are in terms of experiencing church. After I left professional ministry, our family continued attending a church in the area where being "committed" meant being involved in activities on Sunday morning, Sunday evening, Wednesday evening, and often one or two other times during the week related to our respective areas of service or a children's ministry activity. There was also a significant amount of preparation time each week for classes we led or small groups we were in. For the first time I was experiencing the juggling act of life on the other side of the pulpit. Previously I had been paid for all my church involvement, but now that I was working two jobs outside of ministry to make ends meet, it wasn't so easy. We considered ourselves some of the lucky ones who didn't have a thirty-minute drive each way to church.

In time, we left organized church because we felt compelled to focus on developing relationships with a few other families who wanted to experience church on simpler terms. The first obvious difference in being unplugged from organized church was simply having more time. One benefit of this was experienced as a family. With the time gained from not being *at* church, we have found more opportunity to nurture our relationships with each other. We incorporate spiritual times together into our evenings at home when we quietly listen to God together, sing spiritual songs together, share our experiences of God with each other, or toss out a spiritual question for discussion.

Some nights we just hang out listening to music or reading together, playing cards or board games, cooking, playing in the yard, taking walks around our neighborhood, or going places together. This allows plenty of opportunity for conversation. You'd be amazed at what is stirring inside yourself, your spouse, and your daughter when you actually have time and energy to talk about it. The spontaneous talks I have with Pam and Jessica are an important aspect of our journey with God.

We have gotten to know many people in our neighborhood simply by being available. Playing, doing yard work, taking leisurely walks around the neighborhood, inviting folks over for dinner or a party, and taking the time to chat when you catch someone or someone catches you out in the yard or cul-de-sac are ways we have started and developed friendships with people around us. There is more heartache and need up and down these streets than I ever imagined when I used to drive right past them on my way to church. God provides plenty of opportunity to be the church in the midst of doing ordinary life together with others.

Jesus' words "Go and make disciples" (Matthew 28:19) are more accurately translated, "*As you go,* make disciples." In the book of Acts, as Philip is on his way to the city of Jerusalem, he happens across a man who is wrestling with a spiritual matter. One thing leads to another and Philip essentially leads the guy through a Bible study, which opens the man's eyes to the significance of Christ. It's been my own experience that many people I interact with in life express interest in spirituality. God often reveals himself to others through me in conversations and relationships that simply unfold along the way. I've discovered the Spirit still arranges such encounters today as he did with Philip, if I'm open, attentive, and available.

Doing life with neighbors is rather uneventful. It comes down to things like checking in on aged and widowed Ms. Ellie to see if she's getting along okay or to walk her dog, and following the ongoing saga of Tony's (the single guy across the street) love life. There's also Mr. Lawson's mole problem and Brenda's broken garage door. Everyone I've met has a story. Like the little boy missing his dad who is off in Iraq, or the mom who sits alone on her front steps at night and smokes and cries. I know God is present here amid our clogged gutters and Christmas lights that sometimes stay up a little longer than they should.

Last night while walking Jack, the Spirit reminded me that God is in our neighborhood because I carry his divine life within me. I put God and his kingdom in close proximity to others. With God in me, simply being present and available is "ministry." God is already at work in Ms. Ellie's, Mr. Lawson's, and Tony's lives if I will just pay attention. So many people in our neighborhood, as well as all those I've encountered as I go about life, like Wanda the waitress and Mr. Adams the mechanic, have shared their lives with me in simple friendship. Some days I am the kingdom of God for them; some days they are the kingdom of God for me.

I've come to see the significance of my encounters with people is not pointing them *to* God as much as actually being an expression *of* God. The "body of Christ" metaphor has grown in significance for me—that Christ continues his presence and ministry on earth in, through, and as us. The idea of "being Christ" seems a little over the top, until you begin to realize the nuts and bolts of it. We have the same biology and the same life (Christ is our life), just differing expressions of it.

I think we sometimes make things harder than they have to be. I remember once driving to church for an outreach program. We broke up in teams and then were sent off to a neighborhood across town to go "visiting." As I was knocking on some stranger's door, the thought hit me: *Some other church has sent a team of people into my neighborhood, and right now some stranger is knocking on my neighbor's door.* Why don't I just knock on my own neighbor's door and begin a friendship? Talk about accountability—there's nothing like opening up your life to the care and encouragement of someone you can see while standing on your back deck. I guess to some people this idea of church "all the time, everywhere, with everybody" may seem somewhat chaotic, disorganized, or flying by the seat of your pants. Admittedly there's been a time or two I've considered trying to help things along a bit, but I've seen God is capable of working matters out just fine on his own.

Using the illustration of putting new wine into old wineskins, Jesus taught that the implications of his message and ways could not be confined within traditional forms and structures (Mark 2:22). Along with the Mosaic Law, the three central elements of the Old Testament religious system were sacrifice, priesthood, and tabernacle. The radical message of the New Testament, especially the book of Hebrews, is that Jesus Christ is the fulfillment of all three. Jesus is the true and perfect sacrifice, offered once for all; Christ's Spirit within us is now our tabernacle or our connecting place with God; and now our spiritual unity with Christ makes us his "body" or "priesthood"—each of us living and ministering to one another and the world as Christ.

So, for example, church buildings are not essential to the true nature of the church. Christianity has no holy *places*, only holy *people*. Christians did not begin to build church buildings until about AD 200. I'm not saying church buildings are wrong. There are all kinds of practical advantages to having a place where people can gather for any given number of purposes. However, Jesus said "go," or disperse to where people are; but at times our church buildings can reverse it to say "come" to where we are. During its first 150 years, the Christian church had not even heard of church buildings. In those days the church was a mobile, flexible, relational, humble, inclusive reality that spread like wildfire.

If you take the Scriptures as your foundation for constructing your view of church, you have to include what the Greek New Testament calls "koinonia" or "fellowship of the Spirit." In 2 Corinthians 13:14, Paul prays, "May the grace of the Lord Jesus Christ, and the love of God, and the fellowship of the Holy Spirit be with you all." Paul was expressing some essentials of the new wineskin that was to contain the radical spiritual realities of Christ:

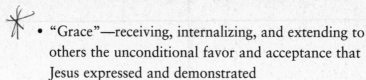

- "Grace"—receiving, internalizing, and extending to others the unconditional favor and acceptance that Jesus expressed and demonstrated

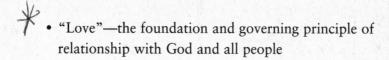

- "Love"—the foundation and governing principle of relationship with God and all people

- "Koinonia" ("fellowship of the Spirit")—the spiritual union of people with God and one another

There are many different aspects of this koinonia concept. For example, if we are unified in the spiritual reality of Christ, then we can be guided and led by that one Christ through the same Spirit within us all. In the early church it was evident in ordinary life and interactions who among them was living spiritual truth day in, day out. These particular individuals naturally emerged as encouragers, teachers, and mentors. However, the risen Christ was given a place of spiritual authority among them that could not be usurped by any man. The teachings and ways of Christ held sway over people's hearts through the leading, guiding, and teaching of the Spirit. The idea of a superstar pastor and staff team does not appear in the Bible. Instead, Paul spoke of the church functioning as a human body, where every person is equally important.

Human nature being what it is, whatever God gets started, man is prone to shape to his own liking. As the number of people actively participating in this new Christ-centered life grew, increasing layers of organization, structure, and leadership were added. The outward reason for the majority of the changes was expediency. I guess it might be judgmental to say there could have been less noble reasons for the move toward more centralization and leadership among these earliest Christ followers. However, it's somewhat conspicuous that each step forward seemed to diminish the spiritual headship of Christ and instead solidified the human governance of men. Perhaps the lesson learned is that any human expedient, regardless of intent, may seem easier at the time but could be contrary to the way of the Spirit.

The way Christianity is now divided up into highly organized denominational systems, with many churches operating under the same organizational model as most businesses, you just figure this is more or less the way it's always been. But that's not true. I read about a movement of Christians in the sixth century who numbered more than two hundred thousand. They functioned as little faith communities scattered abroad without any central authority ruling over them. These communities looked to Christ as their head, and they were built up and strengthened spiritually as they associated with each other. These groups did not have a code of doctrine to which they had to commonly subscribe as a basis for unity. Their spiritual unity lay in the life of Christ, a life manifested in their daily work and relationships.

The more I've been digging around in church history, the more I've seen that the true history of the church often takes its course through the generations of those who were despised by organized Christendom. These Christians were often marginalized, silenced, and deemed heretics. Tragically, sometimes they were killed. As the saying goes, "Only the winners get to write history." My present view of church at times raises the ire of people who believe involvement in some form of institutional church is a litmus test for being Christian. I had many meaningful experiences and met some of my best friends during my years in organized church. I have come to realize all experiences are unique and valuable parts of my journey with God. There are an endless number of ways people conceive of and practice being the church, and I make no claim mine is *the* way. It's just the way for me, and it may be the way for you too. I think we get into trouble when we tout our way as superior. I wish more people felt the freedom to allow their daily lives and interactions to be the means through which Christ brings hope and healing into the world.

Jesus once said that the kingdom of God grows organically. It begins as a tiny and insignificant seed, but then it grows into an enormous tree. If your spiritual radar is on, you will find these little mustard seeds all over the place. Consider, for instance, the conversation I had recently on Rick's boat.

One day I received a phone call from a stranger. The call started this way: "Hey, I'm Rick, and I'm trying to locate a Jim Palmer who posted something yesterday about his journey with God on the Web site TheOoze.com. Is that you?" It was. We agreed to meet for coffee and have been friends ever since. Rick and I began meeting for coffee and conversation on Wednesday evenings or Saturday mornings, sometimes both. Rick had also left organized church, and we were both eager to find someone with whom we would feel free to share our spiritual journey and desire to know God.

Our families also hang out together from time to time; Rick is married with two children in college. My daughter, Jessica, is crazy about Rick and his wife, Heather; and she wants to marry Rick's son, Josh, when she gets older. (Yet another reminder Jessica is growing up—she used to want to marry me!) Rick's daughter, Chelsie, and I seem to be on a similar wavelength. I always enjoy talking with her and the banter that goes on between us. She's a musician, and last Saturday while I was over at their place for breakfast, she got out her guitar and came up with some comedic impromptu songs that had me rolling. Every now and then we stop by their place on a Monday night for dinner, which they host each week for whoever's interested. As I mentioned earlier, everyone on Saint Charles Court knows Monday is spaghetti night at the Harris home. In the winter we hike the trails around Radnor Lake and grab breakfast at Fido's afterward. During the summer we go out on their boat.

One summer evening, Rick, our friend Jeffrey, and I were out on the lake kicking back and talking. Rick said, "Let me roll a question out here that is working its way through me. *Where* do you connect with God in your relationship with him? Where, as in location, is God when you think of him or talk to him? When he's communicating to you, where does his communication come from? Is it the sky—the heaven, clouds, outer space—a sky-God of sorts?" After a couple of moments, Jeffrey responded, "Wow, it's never really crossed my mind before, but think about it. Those dudes in Genesis built that tower *up* into the sky to reach God. And people in church services, at least the ones I went to, reach *up* with their hands during prayer or worship. See what I'm saying? It's always *up*." I chimed in. "Yeah, and think about what every religious professional baseball player does after he smacks a homerun out of the park." We all smiled and pointed to the sky.

So the conversation began on a boat, but then it traveled home with me. That night, as I was lying in bed thinking about it, I asked Pam, "Honey, do you ever think about how people instinctually think of God as being located up in the sky? You know, I envision my prayers beamed up to heaven and then God's answer or intervention comes down from above." After a few moments of silence, Pam replied, "But don't we tell people Jesus 'lives in our hearts'? If so, wouldn't that mean God is located within us?" Pam's response raised a couple of additional questions in my mind. What put this sky-God idea in my head to begin with? And what would it mean to let go of it? So now I have some new questions to add to the mix.

Not long afterward, I was talking to my next-door neighbor, Jeff, out in the driveway, and I said, "Hey Jeff, let me ask you what you think about something. In your mind, where in terms of place do you tend to locate God?" I started asking the same questions to others I came across as I had opportunity. I decided to write a post on my blog about it, and others joined and expanded the conversation.

A few nights later, a few of us Skype our online friend Brian on Rick's laptop. Brian, who lives in New Zealand, normally has a helpful "other side of the world" perspective on things. So what began on Rick's boat now includes my family, neighbors, the gal who cuts my hair, and people scattered across the US and world. It's not a case of folks just sitting around and theorizing interesting concepts about God, but rather people deeply desiring to know God and considering their daily lives and interactions the laboratory for learning and growing.

One Wednesday night at Starbucks, a neighbor of mine listened in on our conversation about the whole sky-God thing and shared how she had discovered that religious people tend to be fearful of God and perhaps that is why they put him in the sky. In other words, out of fear people place God a great distance away. Huh. I wonder what other fears inhibit my relationship with God.

I can't tell you how these kinds of conversations have fueled my desire to know God. It works because it's a no-holds-barred discussion, and nothing is off-limits. We accept each other wherever we are on our journey with God, however messy that might be, but we don't allow each other to get away with too much either. If one of us starts into those religious modes of thinking or drones on in God-talk that has little correlation to our daily reality, we quickly rein things back in.

The *American Heritage Dictionary*'s definition of *conversation* isn't very inspiring: "an informal spoken exchange of thoughts and feelings." For me, it's more like a way of life; it's this living, breathing, essential, invigorating, shaping, vitalizing force. At the heart of this kind of conversation are invaluable questions—the answers to which aren't found on paper but require living your way into them. Even the question "Who is God?" is not adequately answered as the sum total of one's theology or doctrine; you've got to live life with God to fill in that blank.

These people I connect with at different times, in different ways, in different places are midwives assisting me in giving birth to the reality of Christ in my daily life. Their unconditional love and acceptance, the resource of their journeys with God, our ongoing conversation, the example of their lives, their willingness to ask the hard questions and not let me settle, their involvement and help in my life, their support, encouragement, and friendship are all part of helping me become the person God created me to be.

Day by day I'm seeing that under the radar, beneath the surface, and off the grid is a world of nobodies *being* the church. There is very little traction for marketing some sort of church-growth philosophy or strategy from it. It would never occur to my friends to use the word *missional*. We don't have a "strategy" to reach "unbelievers," because these people are simply our friends with whom we spend time and share our lives. Face it, there's not a lot of novelty to having a friend or neighbor over for dinner, going biking, catching a movie or concert together, hooking up for coffee and conversation, arranging a trip to the park for your children to play together, or getting involved in some mutual interest or hobby.

There's no one person or set of persons you can point to as the one(s) in charge of or responsible for what happens. All of us believe that we have an equal "calling" to know God and make him known amid ordinary life and people. Everyone is a leader and a follower, everyone is a teacher and a student, and everyone equally has the fullness of Christ, which is uniquely expressed and offered for the benefit and blessing of all.

In our way of "doing church," you can't click on a calendar and pull up a configuration of services, meetings, and programs. People are compelled by the Spirit to come together in various ways for various reasons and purposes, but these can dissolve, evolve, morph together, and multiply in all sorts of different ways. Our eyes have been opened to our identity as beloved sons and daughters of God and citizens of his kingdom. God is not somewhere up in the sky; he's living his life in and through us, the body of Christ, in the neighborhoods where we live, the places we work and play, and the people we come across each day.

If I had to choose one word to define *church*, it would be *relationships*—relationships with God, one another, and the world, giving birth to the kingdom of God. Whatever kind of church you are led to, my prayer is that you will experience, cultivate, and be transformed by the "grace," "love," and "koinonia" Paul referred to. The fellowship of the Spirit is a spiritual bond that transcends every human form and expression of church. I'm not sure which is more beautiful, our diversity or our unity.

Maybe the saying should go like this:

This is the church, and it is the people,
Grace, love, and one, regardless of steeple.

chapter**four**

Here's to All the Walking Wounded

Is the Bible a Landing Strip or a Launching Pad?

We were at the mall browsing around in stores a couple of days before Christmas when I heard an angry father ripping into his little boy. I looked over and saw the man dragging his son out of the store by his arm. He forced him onto a bench and was unrelenting in his verbal assault as the kid just sat there in a heap of shame. Suddenly a tidal wave of emotion crashed over me. I wanted to cry, I wanted to scream, I wanted to beat the man senseless. Crap. I came so close to making it through Christmas without being tormented by the ghosts of my childhood past. Not this year. Have a freaking merry Christmas!

That night, with those feelings still raw, I felt compelled to write the following blog post:

Here's to all the walking wounded . . .

to those still carrying a little heartbroken boy or girl
   inside;
to those who feel rejected and lonely;
to those who woke up with a dull ache inside;
to those who are wondering where God is in the midst
   of their deep pain;
to those whose past wounds have been pulled opened
   yet again;
to those weary and worn out and longing for some
   place called home;
to those in the darkness who can't seem to find the
   light;
to those who wonder if they will ever find love;
to those who feel misunderstood;
to the abandoned and discarded;
to those who feel they are running out of reasons to get
   out of bed each morning;
to those in the clutches of depression;
to those who are smiling on the outside but dying on
   the inside;
to those suffering in silence.
Here's to all the walking wounded . . .
Merry Christmas.

I received a flood of responses to that blog post—mostly
from churchgoing, Bible-reading Christians who counted
themselves among those walking wounded. Yet Jesus said,
"Come to me, all you who are weary and burdened, and I
will give you rest" (Matthew 11:28). So what's the discon-
nect? Why don't more wounded, hurting, lonely, depressed,
and weary Christians experience this spiritual rest Jesus offers?

I had learned the way you found Christian comfort and peace was reading the Bible. In fact, I often gave people certain Bible verses to memorize as a way of feeling better. But what happens if you grow cold and numb to the Bible and Scripture verses become nothing more than empty words on paper?

Over the years the Bible and I have had a tumultuous relationship. After graduating seminary, I gladly accepted my role as the Bible expert people deferred to when a definitive answer or explanation about God was needed. Through several years of professional ministry, I disciplined myself to rise early each morning to read the Bible. I also spent many more hours each week studying it in preparation for Sunday and Wednesday sermons. The Bible was my road map, my compass, my foundation, my Michael Jordan when the game was on the line with :08 left. No one articulated a higher view of Scripture as the "inspired, infallible, and inerrant Word of God."

However, as life and ministry rolled on, I reached a point where I became increasingly weary and numb to the Bible. Most of the time I read the Bible to learn things *about* God and for gleaning principles for godly living. There were occasional times when I experienced God speaking directly to me through Scripture, but I was trained to approach the Bible in a way and with a process that made it difficult to experience an intimate connection with God. When I read a verse of Scripture, my first task was to determine its original meaning. This might involve the use of various Bible study tools to unpack the contextual, historical, and cultural aspects of the passage. Once I had a firm grasp on its meaning, the challenge was to establish its equivalent meaning for the

present day and circumstances. Eventually, this was all supposed to aid the discovery of some insight about God or how
to live a holy life. Yet God seemed to become more impersonal with each and every step.[11]

As a pastor, I began having ambivalent feelings toward
the Bible, but I suppressed those feelings because of my obligation to study and teach it. Despite this, even after leaving
professional ministry, I maintained a regular time of personal
Bible study. Quite honestly it was simply one of many items
on my daily to-do list, but there was very little joy or meaningful connection with God in it. My negative feelings toward
the Bible intensified as my discovery of God apart from religion continued. After all, it seemed like the Bible was at the
center of my Christian religion, a religion that had left me
empty, exhausted, and disillusioned.

During my process of shedding religion I put away my
Bible for a season, and it's one of the best things I've done
for my relationship with God. I quit reading it. I tuned out
preachers and others quoting or referring to it. Of course, I
had enough horse sense not to broadcast my taking a break
from reading the Bible, but it's not something you can hide
from everyone . . . such as my wife, who was more than a
little concerned.

By the way, if you're just a nanosecond from throwing
this book into the wide open spaces because you can't believe

---

11. It may be that my years of academic Bible study make it more difficult
for me to approach the Scriptures this way without it depersonalizing
God. Pam, on the other hand, would say God speaks to her most often
and most personally through the Hebrew/Greek words she looks up in
her *Strong's* concordance. Obviously, God speaks to different people in
many different ways.

anyone would advocate quitting the reading of Scripture, hang in there . . . I promise it gets better.

The results? God deepened his life in me during my hiatus from the Scriptures in ways I'm still coming to grips with. At the top of the list was the experience of God's unconditional acceptance. For many years I carried inside an unspoken list of "what if" questions about the extent of God's acceptance. I knew God loved me, in a general John 3:16 sort of way, but what if I didn't go to church anymore . . . or have daily quiet times . . . or didn't read my Bible? Would God accept me and love me then? Would I still have a relationship with God then? Would there really even be a God . . . then?

God didn't stop communicating with me when I quit reading the Bible, which took care of several of my "what if" questions. I discovered a living God I could know and interact with in real time whenever I wanted to. The personal and intimate, accepting and loving Father God the Scriptures pointed to was real, *really* real! God began expressing himself in a variety of ways, which I had been oblivious to operating under the assumption that God only spoke through the words of Scripture. These spiritual exchanges between God and me occurred through such things as nature, people, art, film, music, and the still, small voice within.

For me, God went from being locked up in a book that I accessed during morning quiet times, sermon preparation, and Bible study to being everywhere all the time. It's amazing what you can see when you're actually looking . . . and that goes for hearing, touching, smelling, tasting, and feeling as well. It's like God was always there but my radar was off, or only on during specific times and then only narrowly focused in one particular area of Scripture.

Repeatedly bumping into God throughout the day was similar to how you surprisingly see the make and model of your new car everywhere you go. Where were they all before you got that particular car? I have a friend who was telling me he began seeing Jeep Wranglers everywhere after buying one and driving it around. He thinks it's because he's a trendsetter, and everybody in the area saw his and jumped on the Jeep train. I had to break it to him that they were around all the time, but he hadn't been aware of them.

Recently a friend sent me the below brainteaser in an e-mail. Follow the instructions:

Test your eyes
Read quickly and count every "F" in the following text:

FINISHED FILES ARE THE RE
SULT OF YEARS OF SCIENTI
FIC STUDY COMBINED WITH
THE EXPERIENCE OF YEARS . . .
(SEE BELOW)
HOW MANY?

The first time I did it, I only counted three Fs; there are six. The explanation is, there is something about the brain that does not easily process and therefore passes over the word *of*.

In a similar way, religion conditioned my mind to expect God in a fixed number of places, like at church or in my Bible. God was always present and continuously reaching out to me, but I passed right over him. My spiritual brain cannot compute God outside those few avenues. For years I had early morning "quiet times" because I thought of these as my time to "be with God." But then I'd become more or less unaware of God throughout my day until the next morning. Pulling into church, the reality of God was turned on; pulling out, it was turned off. I once was told the rationale for our midweek church service was to remind people about God, because people naturally started forgetting about him a couple of days after the Sunday service. It's like we become dependent on church or the Bible as the spigot of our spirituality and can't seem to tap into God's presence in the natural ebb and flow of life. As the ancient Chinese proverb says, "You never find what you're not looking for."

When I became open to it, communication between God and me began happening more often and was deeply personal. I began turning the attention of my mind and heart to God during my day and found he often had something he wanted to say. He speaks like a father, a friend, a lover, and his words are full of life. He always seems to know when my heart needs comforting or revitalizing insight, a refreshing perspective or encouraging affirmation. I often carry a small journal to record my conversations with God so I can go back and reread them.

I remember one particular journal entry when I was going through a lot of hurt and disillusion. I wrote, "What's going on with me, God? Where am I? Is it a good place? Or is it a deceived and misguided place? I feel so lost, alone, and rejected. This hurts. Have I screwed up? I feel like a fool. What now?" I sat for a while waiting for some sort of response, which never came. I put my journal away and went about my day.

Later that afternoon, I was driving down the interstate

on my way home. At the time, our car's air conditioning was on the blink, so I had the back windows down as I drove along. There wasn't much traffic, a nice breeze was rushing through the car, and I was focused on the road ahead of me. But then I lifted my eyes and was totally swept away by what I saw and felt. Stretched out right before me was an unbelievable deep blue sky, which stood in striking contrast to fields of gold and green farmland that disappeared into the horizon. It was so breathtaking to me, and I felt such peace and freedom looking into those wide open spaces of land and sky.

A few moments passed, and I felt warm feelings of love rising within and God's caring attention turned upon me. God had waited to respond to my earlier journal entry because it was necessary for me to see and feel his answer. God said he was inviting me into his life and that his life would be my freedom, like the freedom I felt looking into the horizon. He assured me that we would step into the future together hand in hand. I didn't record those words of God in my journal, because they are written across my heart and mind.

There was a time when I sought after God because I wanted certain benefits of knowing him. I prayed when I wanted God to give me something or to improve my circumstances in some way. If God created the world in a few days and owned all the cattle on the hills, certainly he could improve my financial situation, guide my steps to a successful career, work out my relationship problems, reduce my stress, get the Hokies to the BCS championship game, and make me feel better every now and again.

Over these past few years, I've experienced a few decisive turning points in my journey with God. One of them occurred during this season when all my Bibles (everyone has more than one, right?) were way back under the couch in my office, intentionally out of view. I was in the midst of sharing life's dissatisfactions with a friend of mine. You know, stuff like: life wasn't working out, I was frustrated with God, and nothing was going right, blah, blah, blah. My friend listened intently—at least I think he was listening intently; he might have been thinking of riding in his Jeep or something. Anyway, he stopped me after a while, and through him God spoke six words that deeply impacted me: "Jim, I AM what you're looking for."

Sometimes I'm not completely sure it was God I heard, sometimes I'm more certain than not, and sometimes I hear God speaking so clearly that it leaves no room whatsoever for doubt. This time I knew it was God, and after a few moments of silence, I understood exactly what God was saying. There's a passage in the Old Testament where someone is inquiring about God's name and God replies, "I AM" (Exodus 3:14). What God was saying to me was, "Jim, you're searching for *it* through life circumstances, human relationships, success, even through a set of Christian beliefs, practices, and principles about me. You seek me because you want me to give *it* to you. Jim, I am *IT*. I am love. I am life. I am peace. I am joy. I am satisfaction. I am freedom. It's not something I give; it's who I am. I AM what you're looking for."

Jesus spoke this truth when he said, "Seek first His kingdom and His righteousness, and all these things will be added to you" (Matthew 6:33 NASB). I missed the order Jesus intended. I was consumed with seeking things instead of letting them be added to my life as a result of seeking God first. One of the most amazing realities of knowing God is finding that knowing God is enough.

This conversation with God was instrumental in my discovering how God makes himself known on different levels or in different dimensions. After all, how are love, peace, joy, and freedom transmitted? Sure you can understand the concept or idea of these things through the mind, but are they experienced purely by the mind? A person may know the definition of *freedom* from the dictionary. They may know how to say "freedom" in thirty-seven languages. They may have read every book ever written on freedom. With all this knowledge they have gathered, they can carry on an intellectual conversation about freedom. But, and it's a big *but*, just because they have knowledge about the topic of freedom doesn't mean they are experiencing and walking in freedom.

Psalm 46:10 says, "Be still, and know I am God." So I began setting aside time to be alone. Often I would seek out nearby sanctuaries of nature. In our neighborhood there are two small wooded areas with a pond and sitting bench. Finding a place that wasn't distracting, I would be attentive to myself—my existence as a spiritual being, and my living and breathing in the container of a human body. I was attentive to my identity in God, a person created in the image of perfect love and lovingly held in God's total acceptance. I was attentive to my surroundings—my place on earth, the ground I was standing on, the air I was breathing, the water in the lake, the warm sun on my face, the trees in the woods. And I allowed my thoughts and feelings to turn toward God in whatever way seemed natural.

Paul wrote in the book of Romans how God expresses himself through creation: "The basic reality of God is plain enough. Open your eyes and there it is! By taking a long and thoughtful look at what God has created, people have always been able to see what their eyes as such can't see: eternal power, for instance, and the mystery of his divine being" (1:19–20 MSG). In my "being still," God expressed himself to me through the sights and sounds of creation.

Observing nature opened my eyes to various spiritual insights, such as like produces like. Orange trees produce oranges, deer produce deer, fish produce fish, humans produce humans. The creation is always the manifestation of the creator. Through this principle of nature, God is continuously encouraging me to see that my essential identity is likewise the manifestation, image, and likeness of my Creator. And who is my Creator? God. Who is God? God is spirit. Therefore, I am more than just my physical biology; I am also a *spirit*ual being. God is love. Therefore, I am love. Sure I might not love at times, but my behavior and attitudes don't create my identity; rather, my identity creates my behavior and attitudes. Whoever a man thinks he is determines what he says and does.

I also observed that all elements of nature fulfill their rightful place by simply being what they are. Trees don't aspire to be fish. They don't even aspire to be better trees. God was saying to me I could experience my rightful place in creation by simply being who he made me to be. This is another one of the most significant discoveries I've come to concerning life in God: life is not about becoming something I'm currently not, but instead being at every moment who I already fully am.

Eventually it occurred to me—whether a conversation in my thoughts; something experienced in silence and solitude; or stimulated by nature, music, film, or art—all these experiences with God were taking place inside of me. It is more than just the presence of God within *giving* me life, but the realization that his presence within me *is* my life. God does not give me peace; he *is* my peace. God does not give me joy; he *is* my joy. This is the kingdom within Jesus was talking about: God in me.

I encountered God in powerful ways even during my religious days, but I was confused as to the true source of those experiences. For example, there were times of corporate worship, the celebration of Communion, and personal Bible reading when some aspects of those activities stimulated the reality of God inside me. I assumed those experiences were only possible during some religious ceremony or from reading the Bible. I became conditioned to believe I had to go to church or read my Bible to experience God. What I didn't realize is the source of those good experiences, thoughts, and feelings was within me and I could also experience God along the daily paths of life. What I needed was for the worship leader to stop in the midst of a moving worship experience and say, "What you are feeling right now inside of you is God. Today as you mow your lawn, that same God will continue to be within you. If you turn your heart toward him, you can experience the love, joy, and peace of God you are feeling now."

As God related to me through all these different means, my desire to know God intensified. One day I was working on something in my office and felt a desire to read the Bible. Honestly, it had been a long time since I *wanted* to read it. Specifically, I wanted to read the Gospels. It took me a little while to remember where my Bibles were—shoved way back under the couch. I pulled one out, turned to the Gospel of Matthew, and began reading . . . and reading . . . and reading . . . and reading . . . and finally had to force myself to stop for dinner.

Once I realized that the point of the Bible wasn't to create a belief system *about* God, the Bible became an invaluable spiritual resource for my journey *with* God. I was shocked to discover what I had been experiencing with God were things Jesus taught and lived. For instance, Jesus was continuously using nature to communicate spiritual truths: a mustard seed, a fig tree, the lilies of the field, the birds in the sky, a kernel of wheat, water, the sun, the wind, the rain. I also saw how Jesus sought out places of silence and solitude for connecting with God. The same unconditional love of God I was experiencing inside, Jesus was continually expressing in the Gospel accounts—to the woman at the well, Nicodemus, the adulterous woman, the centurion, Peter, and others. He even freely associated and offered relationship to some of the most immoral and irreligious people around.

Neither did Jesus have any qualms about opening wide the kingdom of God to everyone. Jesus was continuously emphasizing that it was not necessary to become religious to know God, and that ordinary nobodies were fully capable of knowing and experiencing the reality of God in the context of daily life and living. At one point, a group of religious leaders pressed Jesus about when and how the kingdom of God would come. Surprisingly, Jesus responded by saying it had already come and could be found in and among them.

The more I read, the more things popped out at me. For example, have you ever noticed that the miracle Jesus most often performs is giving sight to the blind? The thought occurred to me, what if this is a message in and of itself? What if Jesus was demonstrating on a physical level something that needed to take place spiritually—the healing of our spiritual eyes? I seemed to be experiencing this miracle right then as I was reading the Scriptures. Previously I only had eyes to see religion in the Bible—a list of dos and don'ts, practices and behaviors, commandments and doctrines. It's like I was conditioned and programmed to read this one way or another into every verse. Even grace passages I turned into "grace but" notions: God loves me unconditionally *but* I better be good, I better obey, I better do this, I better do that . . . or else.

I realized there is much more in the Bible than I was able to see before. I realized it wasn't the Bible that filled me with religion; I had imposed religion upon the Bible and read it into the Bible verse by verse. Once I understood the Scriptures were inviting and guiding me to a deeper experience with God, I became highly motivated to read them. Spending time in the Bible ceased being a religious task I *should* do. The Bible was pointing me to God, and I was taking the bait.

Humankind has a well-established track record for turning what God intends for good into something divisive. The Bible is a perfect example. I realize now my struggles with the Bible were a product of my forcing it to be something it isn't. Is it any surprise the Scriptures inspired by God would function in a similar way as God, existing and expressing himself on different levels and in different dimensions? On one level, the Bible is a story verified through historical facts and evidence. Sometimes the Bible is a long, drawn-out genealogy you're prone to skip over; at other times it's parables, images, metaphors, and poetry that stir something deep within.

At times the Bible tells me more than I care to know about some things; other times it doesn't seem to go far enough. There are occasions when I walk away from the Bible with answers; sometimes I walk away with more questions. I see people in the Bible living the truth, and other times I see them living a lie. Either way I learn something. I once thought of the Bible as a story about people of the past, but now I see it as my own story and seek to understand myself in light of all its characters, situations, and circumstances. God's call to Abraham in Genesis 12 to leave behind everything familiar and comfortable tells me my journey also involves letting go of what's familiar and comfortable in order to experience God's best.

The only real absolute truth is God himself, and our best interpretations of the Bible are only an approximation of it. God was God and Truth was Truth before there was a Bible and will continue on long after the Bible is no more. For years I read the Bible as a way of figuring out how to make God work in my reality; now I see that the Bible is a gift from God designed to pull me into his reality. I no longer think of the Bible as a landing strip for a particular belief system or theology about God, but a spiritual launching pad setting me free to explore and enjoy the height, width, and depth of God's being. There's more in the Bible than meets the eye if you have spiritual eyes to see it. I may have never discovered this if I hadn't stuffed it under the couch for a season. God has cultivated a spiritual openness within me, and if I'm willing, God uses anything and everything to stimulate my spiritual life. Nothing is wasted.

Not too long ago, I was discussing literature with someone who is an avid reader. During the conversation I picked up on the fact this individual wasn't religious and didn't seem to express much interest in spiritual things. Which is why I was surprised when out of the blue he asked me for my opinion of the Bible. Even more interesting, he knew nothing of my own relationship with God. He wanted to know what I thought about the Bible as a book. Here's how I answered: "If tomorrow I was forced to live on a desert island and was told I could only bring one book, the book I would bring with me is the Bible."

After finishing the above paragraph, I decided to go for a run.[12] I must be getting old because while running I experienced short-term memory loss, which, I hate to admit, happens more frequently nowadays. I couldn't remember running through a particular section of the neighborhood and decided to run it again just in case. Eventually I realized through my aching legs and the time, I had run it twice. I was walking a bit to cool down, and while doing so God asked me a question about that desert island.

God said, *Jim, what if on that deserted island you went blind and couldn't see creation or read your Bible? And what if you went deaf and couldn't hear anything either? And what if your memory went bad and you couldn't remember anything about creation or the Bible? Then what?*

Sometimes God asks me a question I already know the answer to. It doesn't happen often, so I milk it for all it's worth. It's his way of allowing us to celebrate the Truth together.

So I played along and said, "Hmm, that's a hard one, God.

---

12. For some reason, running has proven to be an invaluable time for me to connect with God. I can't tell you how many times I began a run with a certain question or struggle, and by the time I got home, a breakthrough of some kind took place in my understanding. It occurred to me once I might work through all kinds of things in the time it would take me to run a marathon. However, then I realized coherent thoughts would cease around mile five, and the rest of the run would be nothing more than irrational hallucinations.

Can't see, can't hear, no memory, hmm . . . Well, you're speaking right now from within me and so even if I was blind, went deaf, and lost my memory, you'd still be there, and I'm sure you'd still be relating to me because you love me."

Anyway, I came up with this new twist on that familiar saying I used to recite about the Bible. Here it is: "This is my Bible: The God it points to is real. The relationship with God it describes I can experience. The God who speaks through it is constantly speaking, if we're listening."

Here's to all the walking wounded. Next time you sink down into those feelings of pain, loneliness, anxiety, rejection, depression, or despair, be still and know there is a real God who meets you in that place and offers love, compassion, acceptance, peace, and freedom.

A Divine Autopsy
Does It Matter WWJD if We Can't Do It?

Recently I came across an Apple Macintosh advertisement in a magazine. It read:

> Here's to the crazy ones. The misfits. The rebels. The troublemakers. The round pegs in the square holes. The ones who see things differently. They're not fond of rules. And they have no respect for the status quo. You can praise them, disagree with them, quote them, disbelieve them, glorify or vilify them. About the only thing you can't do is ignore them. Because they change things. They invent. They imagine. They heal. They explore. They create. They inspire. They push the human race forward. Maybe they have to be crazy.
>
> How else can you stare at an empty canvas and see a work of art? Or sit in silence and hear a song

that's never been written? Or gaze at a red planet and see a laboratory on wheels? We make tools for these kinds of people. Where some people see them as the crazy ones, we see genius. Because the people who are crazy enough to think they can change the world, are the ones who do.

Okay, admittedly I have never invented anything. Let's just say I wasn't the kind of kid curling up with one of those build-your-own-AM/FM-radio kits with capacitors, resistors, transistors, a bunch of wires, and a 9V battery. My mind just doesn't function that way. Heck, I had a hard enough time just putting up our window blinds, and Pam and Jessie made sure they were far away when I did. I may not be inventive, but a few people have tried to pin the words *crazy*, *rebel*, and *troublemaker* on me as a result of asking questions about topics that some Christians feel are simply not open for discussion.

I have discovered the path to God is paved with strange— sometimes threatening and frightening—questions. Typically we assume people who question things, or at least the well-established and widely held things, are "not well-read," are "doubters," or "lack faith." But I've discovered people who ask a lot of questions, particularly the hard ones, often develop a more solid and authentic spirituality and faith. One reason traditional church life is sometimes not a helpful stimulus for spiritual formation is that people are normally rewarded for reinforcing the status quo and frowned upon for upsetting it, which questions often do. Church history is littered with troubling stories of what happens to people who question things.

By now, it's no surprise that I've experienced several bouts of disillusionment these last few years in my journey with God. Disappointment with organized church, Bible burnout, and consternation with Christians, to name a few. But I've carried a sense throughout it all that Jesus Christ came to free me to know God. At the simplest level, I open my heart and apprentice myself to Christ because he helps me know God, which is my desire.

Recently I've been intrigued with how deeply Jesus identifies himself with humankind. Jesus did not immerse himself in the religious establishment and felt at home among the nobodies, even the "sinners." Jesus seemed just as comfortable speaking in the synagogue as he did teaching on a rural hill or in a boat. He worked a day job as a carpenter and lived life among everyday people. Everyone can identify with Jesus' humanity; he experienced joy, sorrow, hunger, love, rejection, temptation, friendship, disappointment, weariness, anger, spiritual struggle, compassion, emotional pain, and physical pain.

What especially began to catch my eye was not identifying with Jesus' humanity but identifying with his spirituality. Jesus matter-of-factly asserted we could all share in his experience of God. In John 17 Jesus prays, "The goal is for all of them to become one heart and mind—just as you, Father, are in me and I in you, so they might be one heart and mind with us. . . . The same glory you gave me, I gave them, so they'll be as unified and together as we are—I in them and you in me. Then they'll be mature in this oneness, and give the godless world evidence that you've sent me and loved them in the same way you've loved me" (vv. 21–23 MSG).

So the same "heart and mind" Jesus and the Father

shared and functioned with is the same heart and mind we can experience and operate with right now. The same "glory," or splendorous identity, of Jesus is our identity. The unity and oneness between Jesus and the Father, we can choose to experience. The eternal flow of love between them includes us in this moment. This spiritual identification even applies to living these truths. Jesus once said, "Anyone who has faith in me will do what I have been doing. He will do even greater things than these" (John 14:12).

This identification of Jesus with humankind is expressed in terms of family in the book of Hebrews: "Since the One who saves and those who are saved have a common origin, Jesus doesn't hesitate to treat them as family, saying, 'I'll tell my good friends, my brothers and sisters, all I know about you; I'll join them in worship and praise to you.' Again, he puts himself in the same family circle when he says, 'Even *I* live by placing my trust in God.' And yet again, 'I'm here with the children God gave me'" (2:11–13 MSG). Jesus and I have the same origin, and he refers to me as his brother.

Seems Jesus of Nazareth, you, me, and the rest of humanity have a lot in common. We share the same biology: Jesus was hungry, thirsty, tired, and subject to physical pain, injury, and death just like the rest of us. We share the same emotional composition: Jesus experienced joy, sorrow, anger, love, and hurt just like the rest of us. Jesus lived within the same space-time dimension of earthly living as we all do; he worked, slept, ate, experienced family and friendship, and faced the same daily challenges and obstacles. He even experienced the same human and spiritual opposition to living truth. Adding to all those similarities, Jesus taught that we share his spiritual reality: his identity in and relationship with God. We all have the capacity to live out these realities on earth as he did.

So why don't we?

What accounts for the discrepancy, or what makes Jesus different from the rest of us? We seem so much alike until it comes down to living out the truth, and then we part ways. Why? This question intensified within me, demanding an answer. Practically speaking, what exactly did Jesus of Nazareth have that I don't have? What specifically makes us different?

What strikes me as an obvious difference between Jesus and the rest of humankind is how he was conceived. Jesus was delivered into this world through a virgin birth; you and I came into this world as a result of regular human childbirth. Why is that such a big difference, practically speaking? Surprisingly, science helped provide an explanation.

Our understanding of the mind-body connection has grown exponentially through research in neuroscience, biochemistry, and genetics. Our brain reacts to numerous stimuli in our environment simultaneously, and it makes decisions on the fly about what things mean and how to respond. It's not necessary to make a new decision in each circumstance because with repeated experience, we form associations. In other words, we learn from our experience, and what we learn colors our response to new situations.

Neuroscience explains that nerve cells are strengthened when stimulated repeatedly, essentially reprogramming the brain to respond accordingly. So ringing a bell each time food is presented causes your brain to associate the sound with food, which produces saliva each time you hear the bell, even if the food isn't presented. You know, like Pavlov's dogs. A neural pathway linking bell and food is established and strengthened through repetition. We've all heard the phrase "Your mind is in a rut." Science explains this physiologically in terms of neural pathways we develop over time, which essentially wires our brain to think and therefore respond a certain way.

Our brains are programmed not only by repeated experiences but also by extreme circumstances. For example, a traumatic experience dramatically alters the brain. Imaging technology allows us to observe the brain in action, showing how trauma actually changes the structure and function of the brain. Research in neurobiology is also finding that our emotions circulate through our bodies as chemicals called neuropeptides, and over time they impact the functioning of the brain as our bodies become addicted to certain emotional states. When repeated experiences generate the same emotional response, our bodies develop an appetite for these types of experiences. Emotional patterns get locked into our brains, and like addicts, we seek experiences that give us our fix.

Neuroscientists believe the brain's foundational patterns and structure are established in infanthood and are significantly influenced through interactions with our primary caregivers. One study combines neurobiology with attachment theory to construct a neurodevelopmental theory of the mind. The theory shows how an infant's interactions may influence the maturation of its brain structure as well as its future socio-emotional functioning.[13]

---

13. My research on neuroscience includes findings from Robert Malenka of Stanford University; Roger Nicoll of University of California; Ross A. Thompson of University of California, Davis; Dan Siegel and Alan Schore of UCLA.

Honestly, reading all this research was rather depressing. I won't even bother getting into all the stuff showing how a malfunctioning mind may be responsible for much of bodily disease. It's amazing anyone ever changes for the better, or even changes at all. It's like the cards (neurons) are stacked against us. The human gene pool producing us is horribly polluted and we are born hazardously hardwired. I've been told before, "Jim, your head's not on straight." The truth is, I was born like that. If that weren't bad enough, before we're out of diapers, we've constructed our basic paradigms of the world, determining how we will live the rest of our lives. Heck, it's pretty much a given: we are created in the image of God, but humanly speaking we are a freaking mess.

Well, that is, unless you are Jesus of Nazareth.

Jesus of Nazareth was not configured or programmed through the human gene pool. Jesus was delivered into human existence through a virgin birth. We share his biology, we share his emotional composition, we share his spiritual identity, we share the same living conditions, but Jesus was born with a fully functioning, uncontaminated, pure, clean, virus-free operating system. No mental ruts, no faulty neural pathways, no preprogrammed mental or emotional patterns passed along by the human genetic highway. Yes, Jesus was born human. He thought with his mind, he felt with his heart, he acted with his will, he faced human conditions and struggles, he embraced and expressed his spiritual identity, but it was all orchestrated through a mind operating on pure truth.

There was a time when I would have said that only twice had someone been born with a perfect mind, never to repeat itself again: the first being Adam and the last, Jesus of Nazareth.

Now I see that Adam and Jesus are meant to represent two choices. Adam set into motion the process that corrupted the mind, and we all see where that led and what that looks like. But Jesus came and initiated a new way. Jesus demonstrated a new kind of human, a God-kind of human, a human being rewired with neural pathways of Truth. Jesus was offering the possibility of a new way when he said, "You will know the truth, and the truth will set you free" (John 8:32).

We've all seen the unsettling antidrug commercials, "This is your brain on drugs," showing teens doing something destructive to themselves or others while high. Adam's message is, "This is a brain on lies." A look back through human history reveals the destructive things the "brain on lies" has led us to do to others and ourselves. Jesus is born into the world and says, "This is a brain on truth." Then he demonstrates what it looks like with his life.

When I first began considering these things, there were times when I wondered if I was meandering down some pointless rabbit trail headed nowhere. Up until then, if I asked any Christian what the difference was between himself and Jesus, the quick and easy answer was, "Jesus is God, and I'm not." Enough said, no further explanation needed, conversation over.

But like a splinter in my mind, I continuously seemed to run into a problem in my Christianity. I told people for many years that the goal of Christian living was to "become like Christ." I even wore a WWJD bracelet to remind me of the key question, "What would Jesus do?" The idea was, at any given moment, I could stop and simply ask the question and the answer would tell me what it meant to be Christian in that particular situation or set of circumstances.

However, there was another aspect of my Christian belief

system that created a huge loophole in this whole WWJD mentality. The loophole was, Jesus is God. I could easily excuse myself from living up to Jesus' example and teachings by simply pointing out that Jesus was God and I wasn't. In one breath I told people to do as Jesus did, and in the next breath I basically told them it wasn't possible. So in the end what I basically did was get myself and others all worked up about achieving the impossible, which only served to produce guilt and shame for not achieving the impossible.

My new question became CADWJD: "Can anyone do what Jesus did?" Jesus answered the question himself in the affirmative and raised the ante by saying, "Anyone who has faith in me will do what I have been doing. He will do even greater things than these" (John 14:12).

So the next question became HHCABGTJ: "How the heck can anyone be greater than Jesus?" This got me wondering, why don't I actually experience this? Eventually this led to WMJMD: "What makes Jesus and me different?" At first it felt like chasing a greased pig, but before long I realized this was the white rabbit God wanted me to follow.

So the main practical difference between Jesus of Nazareth and Jim Palmer is one of birth. Through human birth I entered the world with a horribly flawed operating system, and through virgin birth Jesus entered the world with a perfectly functioning one. What can be done about it now? There's no way I can live up to Jesus' reality with my operating system; I will always fall short. I would have to rewire my brain, effectively reprogramming myself with the same operating system Jesus of Nazareth had. How is that possible?

When I got to HITP: "How is that possible?" I realized I had already come across the answer numerous times without knowing it. I found the answer in Jesus Christ's death and resurrection. The significance of this came in reverse order, the resurrection first. In order for me to truly "be like Jesus," I would essentially have to start over with his operating system. Realizing Christ's resurrection makes this possible, I began seeing the resurrection as an invitation to let go of, or die to, the Adam within me and receive and live a Christ life. By functioning with the new system, I now had the power to put to death the old one. The words *born again* were once just a label used to identify myself as a Christian, but now I realized this was the perfect metaphor and answer to all my questions.

Jesus Christ emphasized the necessity of his physical death as the means of multiplying his spiritual life within people. He is the seed that falls to the ground and dies so it can produce a great spiritual harvest. Realizing this, the apostle Paul wrote, "To them God has chosen to make known among the Gentiles the glorious riches of this mystery, which is Christ in you, the hope of glory" (Colossians 1:27). Suddenly, I realized in a way I never had before that there is a "glorious mystery" to how God is saving me.

What is the mystery? God is saving me from the inside. Our "hope of glory"—our hope for experiencing all Jesus said is possible in our relationship with God—is possible because Christ is "in you." We have Christ's operating system for living the truth Jesus taught and demonstrated. This is why Paul refers to us as "a new creation" (2 Corinthians 5:17) and fleshes it out with statements like "we have the mind of Christ" (1 Corinthians 2:16). Paul described functioning in this reality when he wrote, "I no longer live, but Christ lives in me" (Galatians 2:20). It's not that Christ *gives* us life, but Christ *is* our life and our new operating system. Christian living is not "becoming" something. There isn't anything you lack. God has given you *e-v-e-r-y-t-h-i-n-g* you need for life. You've got it in you.

Now, how do we access it, experience it, live it? Let's go back to science for a minute . . . just a minute, I promise.

Contemporary science is moving toward an insight parents have never doubted: love heals and transforms. As children, a loving embrace could make almost anything better. Neuroscience discovered a reason for this: a primordial area of the brain creates both the capacity and the need for emotional intimacy.

The Institute for Research on Unlimited Love was founded in 2001 with a grant from the John Templeton Foundation. Stephen Post, PhD, professor of bioethics at Case Western Reserve University, leads the institute. The board includes Herbert Benson, MD, of Harvard Medical School, and Edmund D. Pellegrino, MD, professor emeritus of medicine and ethics at the Center for Clinical Bioethics at Georgetown University Medical Center. The institute does research on the effects of love. Not any kind of love, but unselfish and unconditional love without exception.[14] The results are so convincing regarding the impact of love, that Erie Chapman, president and CEO of the Baptist Healing Trust in Nashville, Tennessee, developed an entire approach to health care in hospitals by creating a culture of "loving care." His book *Radical Loving Care* tells the story.[15]

14. For more about The Institute for Research on Unlimited Love, see www.unlimitedloveinstitute.org.
15. Erie Chapman, *Radical Loving Care: Building the Healing Hospital in America* (Nashville: Baptist Healing Trust, 2003).

Scientific research has essentially proven that love heals and transforms. More to the point, that specific aspect of love offering forgiveness is especially powerful. Many painful patterns from the past get locked into our system behind the bars of guilt and shame. As a result, all kinds of negative judgments and self-condemnations multiply within us. The human need for forgiveness emerges from numerous studies demonstrating that unmanaged anger and hostility can be harmful to health.

In other words, our operating system has done a lot of damage to ourselves and others. The most destructive wound this causes is between us and God. We know deep inside we are created as a reflection of God, made in the image of perfect love. But we have violated that image within us and violated that image within others. As a result, guilt and shame cause a sense of separation from God. We go out into the world and seek to meet our need for love, life, worth, meaning, and purpose on the world's terms. We can't come to God and receive these from him because we fear God and feel unworthy of him.

The cross of Jesus Christ was meant to drive the following message into the heart of humankind: God loves you and you are forgiven. We know this in our heads, but it still doesn't change us. Why? Because knowing *about* it isn't enough. The love and forgiveness of God has to get inside of us; we must deeply internalize the love and forgiveness of God in order for there to be any true change. This is one reason "Christ in us" is our hope; the experience of God's love and forgiveness becomes real inside through Christ.

Paul describes it this way: "Because you are sons, God sent the Spirit of his Son into our hearts, the Spirit who calls out, 'Abba, Father.' So you are no longer a slave, but a son;

and since you are a son, God has made you also an heir"
(Galatians 4:6–7). Christ's Spirit within us continuously tells
us, *God forgives you, God loves you, and God is your caring Father.* The bars of guilt and shame are broken, and your
eyes open to the freedom of receiving everything God provides,
including Christ's operating system within you. There is no
separation between you and God, and you can claim the life
of Christ as your own. When John's eyes were open to this,
he proclaimed, "How great is the love the Father has lav-
ished on us, that we should be called children of God! And
that is what we are!" (1 John 3:1).

I used to think the key for living the Christian life was
transferring what I knew up in my head down to my heart.
Now I see it's the reverse: getting what has been deposited
into my heart up into my head. The Spirit of Christ inside
tells me I am forgiven, loved, and a precious child of God.
I've got to allow this truth to transform and renew my mind.
God's love progressively sets me free to function with the
mind of Christ. As Paul wrote to Titus, "For the grace of
God . . . teaches us to say 'No' to ungodliness" (2:11–12). In
other words, as God's unconditional love and acceptance
(grace) frees us to function with Christ's operating system,
we don't "conform any longer to the pattern of this world"—
the old operating system. Instead, our lives "approve what
God's will is—his good, pleasing and perfect will"—the new
operating system (Romans 12:2).

The Christian life is a life operating as Christ. When this
happens we actually, as Peter put it in his second letter, "participate in the divine nature" (1:4). What does this look like
practically? Well, it looks like Jesus Christ. We become like
Christ.

Jesus often said, "Repent, for the kingdom of heaven is near" (Matthew 4:17). I've never liked the word *repent*. For me, it conjures up images of judgment, condemnation, and fear. For years it was troubling to me that Jesus so often used this word, because it smacked of everything about religion that repulsed me. But then I came to understand the true meaning of the word and its significance for my journey with God. The word *repent*, from the Greek word *metanoia*, actually means a change of mind—a radical revision and transformation of our whole mental process. In scientific terms, it would be the equivalent of completely reprogramming the neural pathways and patterns, receiving a new mind.

Jesus taught that *metanoia* was necessary for entering the kingdom of God. In fact, Jesus said, "The kingdom of God is within you" (Luke 17:21). In other words, the kingdom of God is God and everything that derives from him—life, love, joy, peace, grace, goodness, compassion, and freedom. When you repent—change your mind and switch over to the Christ operating system—you become aware of those spiritual realities inside you as well. As you experience these within you, they progressively become what you are in the world, and the kingdom of God becomes a reality "on earth as it is in heaven" (Matthew 6:10).

I've seen this progression play out in the neighborhood where I live. The kingdom of God is present and available through me to everyone here. My first "change of mind" was recognizing that God wakes others up to his kingdom through those who are awake to it already. Sometimes this happens in the most unremarkable ways.

I was asked to serve on the board of our neighborhood

association, and I accepted. At my first board meeting two neighbors came, embroiled in a bitter conflict with each other about a fence. Through the eyes of Christ I could see the greater problem needing resolution was not the issue of the fence, but that these two neighbors harbored resentment and hatred toward each other. A couple of board members applied themselves to working through the specifics of the fence issue, while I focused on helping them see the need for forgiveness and reconciliation.

These last few years I've done a good bit of writing—books, articles, blogs—but one of the most important things I've written lately is our neighborhood quarterly newsletter, a copy of which is taped to the front door of each resident. I was asked to assume responsibility for the newsletter, and my first attempt was a two-paged double-sided and stapled document with articles, news and announcements, and lots of pictures and graphics. In that newsletter you'll learn that our neighborhood-wide garage sale is Saturday, April 16. You'll discover that you can check weather conditions in our neighborhood because Mike set up an official weather station and Web site at his house. You'll find that, yes, we do plan on getting around to repairing the fountain in the back pond. And if you need a recipe for Spanish grilled sandwiches, you lucked out because I included one.

I also sprinkled quotes throughout the newsletter related to the love and peace of God and the beauty of his creation. Oddly enough, no one mentioned the recipe for the Spanish grilled sandwiches (except Mr. Hamilton, who said they sounded nauseating), but several people made a point to say how they appreciated the quotes. A quote in a newsletter doesn't seem like much, but Jesus pointed out that God things often come in small packages. A newsletter taped to a door containing one sentence of truth can breathe hope into a hurting person and influence her next thought or action. Maybe that action is saying thank you to the person who put the quote in the newsletter, which leads to a conversation, which leads to a friendship, which leads to . . .

The more I receive and depend on the unconditional love and acceptance of God, the more my old operating system seems to fall by the wayside. The more I function with the Christ operating system, the more I experience the present reality of God's kingdom within me. The more I experience the present reality of God's kingdom within me, the more I give earthly expression to it in my thoughts, feelings, words, and actions in everything I do. What God asks of me is to abide or remain in his love. The fruit of this abiding is a reprogramming of Jim Palmer. This Jim thinks with the mind of Christ, feels with the heart of Christ, sees with the eyes of Christ, and acts with the will of Christ.

There's this river. For years I walked its banks and from time to time I would go to the edge and peer into the water to see a reflection of myself. A stupid, ugly, worthless little kid looked back at me and I walked away from the water hurting inside. That useless kid was never going to invent, imagine, heal, explore, create, or inspire. I said to myself, "Yes, I am stupid, ugly, and worthless."

One day Christ took my hand and led me back to the water's edge. He said, *Look, Jim.* I gazed into the water and surprisingly saw someone different: a magnificent, loved, accepted, and powerful man. I said to myself, "This can't be me." Then suddenly I realized I was not looking into that same old river. I was now looking into the eyes of God and seeing a reflection of myself in the pupil of his eye. The reflection was the "me" God was seeing in his mind.

At some point you've just got to grow up and become who you really are. It's not a matter of figuring out "what would Jesus do?" but living your identity in and as Christ. Now I know the truth. I have become crazy enough to think I can change the world. What's stopping me? I've been reprogrammed as Christ. That rebel from Nazareth is now me.

chapter six

The Devil Wears Levis 501 Jeans

Is the Reality of Evil an Inconvenient Truth?

I don't see my memory ever letting go of the horrific events that transpired on April 16 and 17, 2007. It was a Monday when Pam called me at home and asked in a somber voice, "Have you heard?" "Heard what?" I replied. She told me to turn on the television, which I did, discovering that a massacre had taken place on the Virginia Tech campus in Blacksburg, Virginia, where I grew up. Seung-Hui Cho, age twenty-three, an English literature student, gunned down thirty-two students and professors before killing himself, the deadliest college campus killing in history.

When Pam called, I was wearing my VT baseball hat—nothing unusual as I wore it quite a bit, but sobering in this instance. Suddenly I was seeing on television all the places I hung out as a kid. There's not a whole lot to do in the small town of Blacksburg, and Virginia Tech supplies all the excitement. I saw the War Memorial Coliseum, where I used to play pickup games of basketball; and Lane Stadium, where I saw an endless number of Hokie football games; and the student center, where we used to go play pool and eat doughnuts. Blacksburg is a close-knit community, and a tragedy of this magnitude will be a painful scar in the hearts of many for a long time to come.

When I woke up on Tuesday, April 17, I checked the news on my laptop for a Virginia Tech update and was confronted with another gruesome set of events, not in Blacksburg but in Baghdad. The story read, "One car bomb alone in the mainly Shi'ite Sadriya neighborhood killed 140 people and wounded 150, police said, making it the worst insurgent bomb attack in Baghdad since the US-led invasion in 2003. 'The street was transformed into a swimming pool of blood,' . . . a shopkeeper near the scene told Reuters. . . . 'Women were screaming and shouting for their loved ones who died,' said the witness who did not wish to be identified, adding many of the dead were women and children."[16]

As I continue on in my journey with God, some answers I unquestioningly accepted back in my religious days don't seem to ring true anymore. If the Virginia Tech tragedy had taken place three years ago, I would have responded by saying things like, "God knows and cares," "They are in our prayers," and "God is on our side and Satan will not prevail." In the days that followed, the focus turned to Seung-Hui Cho, his background and psychological problems, and his possible motives for the killing. The more I read, the

---

16. Dean Yates and Paul Tait, "Bombs kill nearly 200 in Baghdad after PM's pledge," Reuters, 18 April 2007.

more I began to feel the focus was a diversion from addressing this evil on a deeper level.

There's a battle in the world between good and evil. We all
know the source of goodness is God, no problem there. But
what about evil? Who or what is the source of evil? Isn't it
logical that in a good-versus-evil battle, you must confront
the source of evil and not just its symptoms? Seung-Hui Cho
pulled the trigger, but what made him do it? Terrorist insurgents
wage war in Baghdad. What motivates this violence? For many
years, the way I would have answered these questions could be
summarized as follows: "Satan made them do it." To me, Satan
was the source of evil, and so ultimately you could trace it all
back to him. In my mind these people were possessed by Satan,
if perhaps only temporarily, to do these vile and despicable acts.

So I thought, *How do you confront evil at its source and
fight Satan?* Which raised another question: *Who or what
exactly is Satan?* Through religious conditioning, I was prone
to locate spiritual realities outside myself. But little by little I
was discovering them inside. Here are some examples:

Then: God is up in the sky.
Now: God dwells within me.

Then: I go to church to meet with God.
Now: God's presence is inside me.

Then: Christianity is me trying to be like Christ.
Now: Christianity is Christ's life in and as me.

Then: The benefit of knowing God is the love, joy, and
peace God brings into the circumstances of my life.

Now: God inside me is my love, joy, and peace.

Then: Pastors, leaders, and teachers guide, teach, and train me.
Now: The indwelling Spirit is my primary teacher.

Then: Changing my behavior is the goal.
Now: A new mind and heart is what God provides.

Then: People are as they appear in their physical human identity.
Now: What's most true about a person is his or her invisible spiritual identity.

Then: The kingdom of God will one day come down onto earth.
Now: The kingdom of God exists now within me.

If spiritual reality is within me, it seems logical to wonder if perhaps the real spiritual battle is also within me. When the Bible speaks of the end times, it often alludes to an epic battle that takes place between the armies of the north and south. Maybe this is the battle between my head (north) and my heart (south). If so, I was going to have a real problem with a billboard I saw driving through Kentucky that had a huge picture of a Bible and the words, "A Chapter a Day Keeps the Devil Away." The message was clear: my adversary is Satan, and my mission is to keep him away.

I'm a scaredy-cat, which is why I don't shell out eight bucks for a horror movie that will have me so frightened I'll gladly take forty-five minutes to go to the bathroom and get my tub of popcorn refilled. It also gets tiring standing in the rear of the theater with a wall at my back so as to protect my hind side from a surprise attack.

The first horror movie I ever saw as a kid was an old Steve McQueen movie called *The Blob*. The blob is this mass of evil jelly that lands on earth and proceeds to engulf and eat everything it can get its slimy little mouth on. You're pretty much not safe anywhere, not even leaning against the wall in the back of the theater. You can lock your door and windows, but before you know it, the blob is oozing out of the air conditioner vent. Needless to say I still stay far, far away from air conditioner vents.

The next horror movie I saw was *Jaws*, after which I refused to take baths; it was a shower or nothing. Now I don't have to even watch a horror movie—just seeing the trailers messes with me. I made the mistake of watching the trailer for the film *The Hills Have Eyes*. Now, whenever I take the trash out at night, I make it quick; there's no way I'm risking some bitter mutant dragging me off to perform horrendous experiments.

Which brings me to Satan. My image of Satan was a conglomeration of the Bible and Hollywood. In a nutshell, Satan was someone to be feared more than Freddy, Jason, and Hannibal Lecter combined. Movies such as *The Exorcist* contributed to my overall sense of Satan as a lurking evil presence seeking to destroy me. I still vividly remember being in Bible studies, trying to sort out the difference between Satan and his demons "possessing" non-Christians and "oppressing" Christians. Either way, Satan "prowls around like a roaring lion looking for someone to devour" (1 Peter 5:8).

I also attributed spiritual struggles, destructive thoughts, and behaviors to the influence and trickery of Satan. Just getting to the end of a day was no small feat, since I was convinced that Satan had planted all kinds of land mines and traps along my path to lure me into evil. My defense against Satan involved faithfully fulfilling a regimen of spiritual disciplines and boning up on Bible verses to withstand his attacks.

As my relationship with God grows more intimate, his qualities of love, joy, peace, freedom, and compassion intensify inside me and change how I live in the world. Equally so, opposing inner qualities, such as fear and insecurity, seem to fall away. In a nutshell, the more I experience God's unconditional love and acceptance, the less I fear. The more I trust God's perfect love, the less I fear letting go of old boxes and mentalities. The more I embrace my spiritual identity, the less I fear being a nobody in the world. The more I experience God's freedom, the less I fear criticism and rejection of others.

A MySpace friend was wondering what life would be like if we had no fear. What got her thinking about it was 1 John 4:18, which reads, "There is no fear in love. But perfect love drives out fear, because fear has to do with punishment. The one who fears is not made perfect in love." Another translation says, "There is no room in love for fear. Well-formed love banishes fear. Since fear is crippling, a fearful life—fear of death, fear of judgment—is one not yet fully formed in love" (MSG).

Speaking of billboards, those words formed one in my mind: "No Fear in Love! Perfect Love Drives Out Fear!" Reflecting upon these words, the subject of Satan came to mind. Should I fear Satan? If God is perfect love, is there any room left for the fear of Satan, or does the perfect love of God within me banish the fear of Satan? And if so, how? If

Satan is real, it seems that we should fear him. After all, isn't some fear beneficial? If Satan is constantly working to hinder and obstruct my experience of God's kingdom by laying evil traps each step of the way, he should be feared . . . right?

Paul wrote in 1 Corinthians 2:14–16: "But the natural, nonspiritual man does not accept or welcome or admit into his heart the gifts and teachings and revelations of the Spirit of God, for they are folly (meaningless nonsense) to him; and he is incapable of knowing them [of progressively recognizing, understanding, and becoming better acquainted with them] because they are spiritually discerned and estimated and appreciated. But the spiritual man tries all things [he examines, investigates, inquires into, questions, and discerns all things] . . . But we have the mind of Christ (the Messiah) and do hold the thoughts (feelings and purposes) of His heart" (AMP). According to this passage, we have a "nonspiritual" self that has no capacity for knowing God and operates on purely human terms, and we have the "mind of Christ" that transmits the feelings and purposes of God in our hearts. Can you see the conflict?

The nonspiritual self will have nothing to do with the "gifts and teachings and revelations" of God. The nonspiritual self has a mind of its own and wants to operate accordingly in its human consciousness, reasoning, and rationalizations. Think about the words the Bible uses to describe Satan: "deceiver," "accuser," "liar," "killer," and even an "angel [messenger] of light." Isn't that what our human mind does to us? It deceives us into thinking the good life is worldly gain and status, it accuses our hearts of being unworthy and unacceptable to God, it lies to us about what will bring true peace and freedom, it steals our joy—and yet we listen because it speaks as "an angel of light" and seems so convincing. The English word *demon* in Scripture is literally translated as a god or deity. So these deceits, accusations, and lies are an authority that when given a place in our lives, can rule over us.

When our nonspiritual self is in control, bad things happen. The Bible warns, "Don't let anyone under pressure to give in to evil say, 'God is trying to trip me up.' God is impervious to evil, and puts evil in no one's way. The temptation to give in to evil comes from us and only us. We have no one to blame but the leering, seducing flare-up of our own lust. Lust gets pregnant, and has a baby: sin! Sin grows up to adulthood, and becomes a real killer" (James 1:13–15 MSG).

A few chapters later, James illustrates practically how this internal conflict plays out: "Where do you think all these appalling wars and quarrels come from? Do you think they just happen? Think again. They come about because you want your own way, and fight for it deep inside yourselves. You lust for what you don't have and are willing to kill to get it. You want what isn't yours and will risk violence to get your hands on it. You wouldn't think of just asking God for it, would you? And why not? Because you know you'd be asking for what you have no right to. You're spoiled children, each wanting your own way" (4:1–3 MSG).

Simply, the conflict and chaos in the world corresponds to conflict and chaos within us. Maybe the greatest deception is our making this separate personality (Satan) to blame (a scapegoat), which in effect takes the focus off of us where the blame belongs. It all begins as an inner spiritual battle, which takes shape in our outward actions and human relationships. Paul describes this spiritual battle as a conflict between the "Spirit" and "flesh." He writes in Romans 8:5, "Those who live according to the flesh have their minds set on what that nature desires; but those who live in accordance with the Spirit have their minds set on what the Spirit desires" (NIV-UK).

If these conflicts and battles are within me, between my unspiritual and spiritual self, my battle is *not* with Satan but with myself. The capacity to go out into the world and wage war is inside me. Satan didn't "make me do it." I did. It doesn't take Satan under cover of night to deceitfully lure me into hate, perversion, and violence. I am capable of all of this and more in broad daylight. Jesus pointed this out when he said things like, "You're familiar with the command to the ancients, 'Do not murder.' I'm telling you that anyone who is so much as angry with a brother or sister is guilty of murder" (Matthew 5:21–22 MSG). In other words, the outward act of murder stems from anger within us. Never underestimate the hideous possibilities of a mind operating out of the nonspiritual self.

This shift of understanding in terms of my real "spiritual battle" has liberated me in several ways. First, it freed me from fearing Satan. God would not send me into the hills if the hills had eyes and some evil creature was waiting to jump out and get me. The hills don't have eyes, and the creature is inside me and not nearly as imposing—it's me. Sure, I can be pretty scary, and as Jesus and others pointed out, I am capable of the worst evil, but the difference is a pretty simple solution: live from the Spirit. In other words, I am not defenseless and at the mercy of some evil *out there*. There's freedom in realizing the boogeyman is my own desire to be like God. This realization helps us to know who's fighting and where the fight is. Jesus came to set the captives free . . . free from ourselves.

I've done missionary work in the most remote places in Africa and Thailand. While there, I met people who were enslaved to the most hideous lies. When they finally recognized the truth that could set them free, some people even experienced physical sensations of being released. They felt like their chest was being ripped open, began choking, and fell to the ground. When I traveled with the International Justice Mission, I saw some of the most grisly human rights violations against humankind. But human beings committed these crimes. There's no question that evil is real, but I have never found any other solution in overcoming it other than depending on the Father and living in the truth.

Perhaps the most helpful discovery about this battle within is that it's really not a "battle" at all, or at least not one fought in conventional terms. It's not about trying to overpower or eliminate the nonspiritual self; I just live out of the spiritual self, who is one with God, and the nonspiritual self ceases to exist. As I depend on God for my worth, meaning, acceptance, significance, and purpose, and as I experience God as my love, life, peace, joy, and freedom, I have no need to seek these things in the world through pride, hate, greed, manipulation, domination, deceit, and lust.

Slowly but surely, that old nonspiritual self is dying and I have little need or use for him. The law of sowing and reaping says that if I live my life out of the nonspiritual self, I will reap accordingly—hate, discord, conflict, weariness, anger, bitterness, and dissatisfaction. If I live from my spiritual self, I reap love, joy, peace, and fulfillment within regardless of my circumstances. I will then allow these qualities to over-flow into daily living and my relationship with others.

This perspective also protects me from the diversion of blaming Satan for my present reality and investing in some scheme for fighting Satan, which averts my attention from the illusions and lies within me. In other words, I excuse myself from facing the disturbing truth that I am not think-ing and acting out of the reality of who I really am in Christ. Sure, it's not a very nice thought that I'm to blame for evil and suffering in the world. On the other hand, if I'm to blame, I can change it. Leo Tolstoy once said, "Everyone thinks of changing the world, but no one thinks of changing himself."

I wrestled long and hard with the question of who or what Satan is. Is Satan a personal being with a physical form, or is Satan a system or energy distracting us from the truth and reinforcing false beliefs that enslave and rule over us? I've never encountered Satan as a personal being, but I can vouch for the latter.

I have believed all kinds of lies, which have enslaved me and poisoned my relationships and prevented me from walk-ing in the freedom God desires for me. My head said, "Jim, you are one colossal failure and your life is a waste. You bet-ter get busy and try to turn this around! Do something! Accomplish something huge! You are not worthy of love and too defective to be accepted as you are. Seek love, accept-ance, meaning, and worth any way you can get your hands on it." But the voice of God in my heart said, *Jim, you are a person of magnificent beauty and worth. I unconditionally love and accept you just as you are, no changes needed or required. You are perfect to me. Rest.* I had a choice: listen to the lie in my head or the truth in my heart. That evil lie in my head almost destroyed my life. Listening to the voice in my heart is saving me.

If "Satan" is the human consciousness, which rationalizes and reasons desiring to be like God, I can say that Jesus stared down these tempting lies and overcame them. Jesus said, "I tell you the truth, the Son can do nothing by himself; he can do only what he sees his Father doing, because whatever the Father does the Son also does" and "I do nothing on my own but speak just what the Father has taught me" (John 5:19; 8:28).

The sinful nature is the nature of someone who is guided by the human consciousness rather than by the Father as Jesus was guided. Jesus didn't have a sinful nature because he didn't sin; his nature was 100 percent holy, righteous, and pure because of his ability to conquer "Satan" using the above method—total dependence on the Father. What an encouragement that Jesus battled and defeated the same human consciousness ("Satan") that I battle. Especially given that Jesus is my life and can defeat Satan's temptations in me the same way . . . if I choose to depend on him.

The Virginia Tech tragedy strengthened my resolve to live the truth—to walk more boldly as a man created in the image of perfect love. There's a certain grit or muscle to love that you develop over time. That muscle is tattooed with a big VT on it.

chapter seven

For the Least of These

Are We Too Religiously Minded to
Be Any Earthly Good?

I'm in my garage writing while Jessica is inside playing with Shayna, one of her regular playmates. Shayna's family is from India, and they have been good friends of ours going on five years now. Matavee, Shayna's mom, likes giving us Indian food, which works out great since I like eating it. Whenever Jessie goes over to their house to play, Matavee makes an extra helping of whatever she is preparing for dinner that night and sends it home with Jessie. Last week I took Jessica to Shayna's birthday party and hit the jackpot with plates and bowls of authentic Indian cuisine everywhere!

Once a week I teach a world geography class to a group of teenagers in a local homeschool co-op. When we studied the continent of Asia, I invited Matavee to come and tell the class about her childhood and youth in India. Matavee and her family are Hindu, and I asked her to share about this as part of her presentation. All the students are from Christian families and I felt it would be beneficial for them to hear someone share different religious beliefs than their own.

Matavee began her presentation by addressing the class with a common Hindi greeting, "Namaste." The word is often used as a general acknowledgment like "hello," but Matavee went on to explain the word also has a notable spiritual meaning. Translated into its spiritual significance, *namaste* means something along the lines of: "The image of God in me honors the image of God in you. I recognize that you and I are equal in God's eyes. I greet you in that place where you and I are one."

After class, I pondered what Matavee had shared. Our world is filled with people who differ in race, culture, socio-economic class, politics, and religious beliefs. These differences are sometimes the cause of bitter, even bloody conflict. So what is this place that the namaste greeting identifies where we all are "one"?

There are certain aspects of God that every religion agrees on, like God's compassion for "the least of these." In Matthew 25, Jesus identifies the act of aiding those in need as a defining characteristic of someone tuned into God's kingdom. Jesus says, "I was hungry and you fed me, I was thirsty and you gave me a drink, I was homeless and you gave me a room, I was shivering and you gave me clothes, I was sick and you stopped to visit, I was in prison and you came to me." Jesus' use of the word "I" throws everybody off, and they respond, "Master, what are you talking about? When did we ever see you hungry and feed you, thirsty and give you a drink? And when did we ever see you sick or in prison and come to you?" Jesus answers, "Whenever you did one of these things to someone overlooked or ignored, that was me—you did it to me." (vv. 35–40 MSG).

Compassion is also taught in Islam. Early historical accounts say the prophet Mohammad never turned anyone away empty-handed from his house and always gave preference to the needy over his own needs. The Koran says, "Righteousness is this: that one should . . . give away wealth out of love for Him to the near of kin and the orphans and the needy and the wayfarer and the beggars and for the emancipation of the captives" (2.177). Likewise, Buddha taught that the practice of compassion could introduce you to Nirvana. Once at Matavee's home I picked up a Hindu magazine and read, "The Hindu of the future must be confident about the worth of the Hindu heritage, but dedicated to the idea of an active, self-sacrificing love."[17]

Judaism also emphasizes compassion and seeking justice for the oppressed. The Jewish Scriptures read, "Break the chains of injustice, get rid of exploitation in the workplace, free the oppressed, cancel debts. What I'm interested in seeing you do is: sharing your food with the hungry, inviting the homeless poor into your homes, putting clothes on the shivering ill-clad, being available to your own families. Do this and the lights will turn on, and your lives will turn around at once. Your righteousness will pave your way. The GOD of glory will secure your passage" (Isaiah 58:6–10 MSG).

It's likely you have heard the saying, "In essentials, unity; in nonessentials, liberty; in all things, charity." The quote is

---

17. Anantanand Rambachan, "Hindu Pride or Hindu Arrogance?" *Hinduism Today*, October 1988, available at http://www.hinduismtoday. com/archives/1988/10/1988-10-08.shtml. Accessed 7 June 2007.

said to have originated with Augustine. At first glance, the idea seems to hold promise for encouraging people of differences to work together in order to help others in need. Unfortunately, religious people like to focus on the first part of the quote: "In essentials, unity." To the religious mind, this gives permission to insist on a doctrinal creed for the basis of unity and to refuse association with those who differ.

As I have grown more intimate with God these past few years, my "essentials" have changed from theological doctrines about God to the passions of God for the world. As Bono pointed out, "This is not a Republican idea. It is not a Democratic idea. It is not even, with all due respect, an American idea. Nor is it unique to any one faith."[18] In other words, alleviating the sufferings of our world is not an idea original to any political party, country, or religion. They surface in all of them because this is God's desire, which we all carry as living images of God.

Mother Teresa, Martin Luther King Jr., William Wilberforce, and Gandhi were simply expressing what is hardwired into each of us as human beings. They identified the love of God as their motivation for serving others in need and confronting injustices in the world. Jesus himself said love for God and love for people are inseparable. Maybe that's the "essential" we should be focusing on. It seems to be the essential that the Bible emphasizes. As the apostle John wrote, "My beloved friends, let us continue to love each other since love comes from God. Everyone who loves is born of God

---

18. Bono, "Justice and Equality Are Neither Republican Nor Democratic," speech at the 2006 National Prayer Breakfast, available at http://usliberals.about.com/od/faithinpubliclife/a/BonoSermon_3.htm, accessed on 28 May 2007.

and experiences a relationship with God. The person who refuses to love doesn't know the first thing about God, because God is love—so you can't know him if you don't love" (1 John 4:7–8).

Too often, religion becomes so preoccupied with self-preservation that its adherents lose touch with their spiritual identity as the heart, hands, and feet of God in the world. Like the religious men in Jesus' parable of the Good Samaritan, we are in such a hurry to get to church that we pass right by a sea of suffering people. The old saying, with one slight modification, seems to fit, "We are so ~~heavenly~~ religiously minded that we are of no earthly good." The world notices this. Like my atheist friend Reginald, who told me once that the phrase "I'll pray for them" is code language for "Don't ask me to get involved."

One Sunday morning while reading the Nashville newspaper, I came across this headline: "Plight of the Kurds." The story was about how thousands of Kurdish immigrants forced from their homeland are now living in Nashville. Turns out, the Kurdish population in Nashville is consistently in the top two or three in all the United States. Reading along, the Spirit prompted me to call the phone number listed for anyone interested in helping serve these refugees in some practical way.

Making the call put me in contact with an Iraqi woman living in Nashville named Nihad. She explained to me that there was a significant need among the Kurds for English tutoring. I agreed to meet Nihad at the home of a particular Iranian family who needed this help. The father of the family was struggling to find good employment because he could not speak English well. I drove down to the south side of

Nashville and met Nihad in the parking lot of their apartment complex. When Nihad knocked, the father opened the door, and I stepped into a world I was largely ignorant of.

Once inside their tiny apartment, Nihad introduced me to the entire family, which included the mother and father, their young son, and their infant daughter. It was difficult to concentrate as I was noticing cockroaches crawling up and down the walls. We sat at a table in the dining area from which you could see the rest of the apartment—the front room, kitchen, and a couple of bedrooms. While Nihad translated conversation between us, the mother stepped into the kitchen to pour hot tea for us all. When she picked up a spoon on the counter, a huddle of roaches scurried off.

I began meeting with the father, Nasrallah, once or twice a week in their apartment to tutor him in English. It made for some interesting evenings at first, as he knew virtually no English and I knew absolutely no Parsi, but we got through it (barely). A few times Pam and Jessie joined me.

One week when I arrived, their apartment was flooded with water from a busted pipe in the above apartment. It had been that way for three days. The apartment owners could only be reached by phone, and Nasrallah was not confident enough in his English skills to place the call. Instead, they had towels spread out trying to soak the water out of the carpet and were not able to use their kitchen. On another occasion he showed me their phone bill, which included several significant charges on features they didn't use or need. These kinds of things were simple for me to take care of for them. In short order, their water problem was resolved and their phone bill adjusted.

As Nasrallah and I began trusting each other, a friendship developed and we shared food and music with each other. We also shared photographs of the significant people, places, and happenings of our lives. Seems like each week I was meeting another family member—brothers, uncles, nieces, and nephews. Though Nasrallah is Muslim and I a Christian, we started praying together. After each English lesson before parting, we stood at his kitchen table and said a short prayer asking God to bless the other. I felt God's pleasure during these times. Sometimes his wife would join us, and we would hold hands as we prayed.

What I'm discovering is that after you skim off every religion's 5 percent of extremists and fanatics (including Christians), the remaining 95 percent from each group care about the same things: peace, justice, family, health, dignity, and basic necessities for living. In Luke 6:31, Jesus said, "Do to others as you would have them do to you." The implication seems obvious.

If you were starving to death, you would want someone to feed you.

If you were dying of thirst, you would want someone to give you water.

If you were suffering under the abuse of an oppressor, you would want someone to rescue you and remove the oppressor.

If you were dying from disease, you would want access to medical care.

If you were not capable of providing for your own needs, you would want someone's support to help you get there.

If you had suffered for years under abuse, you would want a caring and loving person to help nurture you back to wholeness.

I sometimes contemplate this regarding my daughter, Jessica. If any of these things were true of her and I was not able to help her myself, I would desperately hope someone, anyone, would provide for her need. Maybe this is a place where the spiritual meaning of namaste applies. I can look into the eyes of my worst enemy and say, "I greet you in that place where we are one in wanting our daughters to be safe, healthy, and free."

Jessica once had a soccer game against a team that was coached by a Middle Eastern man. Most of the kids on the team also appeared to be of the same descent. As the assistant coach of Jessica's team, I met and had some interaction with the guy. Frankly, I didn't care for him. He seemed somewhat abrasive and arrogant. It didn't help that his team demolished us. A couple of their moms on the sidelines were covered head to toe in traditional Muslim garb. I began having negative and judgmental feelings toward them—the coach, the women, all of them.

We hung around for a while after the game, and as we were leaving I spotted that coach loading up his own vehicle with soccer gear. Then I noticed his wife walking over to the car with a little boy. It was evident the boy had severe developmental disabilities. The boy was excited to see his dad and let out all kinds of animated grunts and groans. The coach gathered up his son into his arms and kissed him. My negative and judgmental thoughts about the man left me, and all I could feel for the man was compassion and love. In that moment, the man was not my enemy, the man was not Muslim, the man was not the coach that just demolished my daughter's team— he was just a man who loved and cared for his disabled son. I realize now I was feeling the heart of God for this man.

The value of a person to God is not determined by what percentage of his or her theology is correct. When I was in Africa, I met a woman who had infected her child with HIV/AIDS, which will end both their lives. Does God turn his head to their suffering because the mother and child have no religious creed? When I was in Asia, I met a little girl who had been forced into child prostitution and was being raped three or four times a day, six days a week. Do not Christians, Muslims, and Jews all agree this grieves the heart of God? One evening, while I was executive director of an inner-city agency in Nashville, we received a phone call from an employee at a Mapco down the street. She told us two young boys had wandered in and had no place to go. Their mother's cocaine-addicted boyfriend had beaten them and locked them out of the house on a frigid winter's night. The boys walked a couple of miles barefoot to the Mapco for help. Does anyone's doctrine teach that we should not come to their aid?

There have been a few times these past few years when I almost became so "spiritual" that the suffering of our world became acceptable. One perspective says that people suffer as a necessary part of their journey and that intervening would violate the process. I can attest to the fact that, although God is not the source of pain and suffering, he can use it as part of the process of my growth and transformation. However, I would be hard-pressed to explain to the little girl forced into prostitution and held captive in a brothel that it wouldn't be wise for me to rescue her since her abuse is just part of the journey. Even if I see an injured dog on the side of the road, I feel compassion and compelled to come to the animal's aid.

Whenever I start drifting into my spiritual sophistication, I am often prompted to remember Jesus Christ, who was not of this world and yet laid down his life for it. Jesus said in John 17:18, "As you sent me into the world, I have sent them into the world." Jesus was continuously in compassion mode. Whether it was spiritual deception or blindness, physical disease, the systemic victimization of the poor, or even a shortage of wine at a wedding, Jesus was motivated to intervene.

I've discovered my heart is elastic, and God keeps stretching it further in compassion for a greater number of needs in our world. I've reached this point where it matters not who I might partner with in order to assist others in need. Recently, I was serving meals at a homeless shelter alongside a Jewish man. It hit me that we both were bearing witness to our shared understanding of God's love and compassion for "the least of these." Through our simple interactions with each other, we were experiencing the image of God in the other, expressed through our distinct human personalities and our common spiritual compassion. We found that place where he and I are one. More and more in my encounters I look for that place.

Let's face it: most of us are not Bono, with his kind of cash, clout, and connections. What I'm finding for myself is that as I'm consciously aware of God's love for me, it overflows in love for the world. It's as if my spiritual radar is alerting me to people I have opportunity to help in some way. It was this sensitivity that drew my attention to the story in the newspaper concerning the plight of Nashville's Kurds. Often the outcome of such promptings is coming to the service of someone in need by practicing the gifts and talents God has given us. For example, Lisa, one of Pam's friends who is a licensed massage therapist, goes to the Nashville shelter for women and gives free massage therapy to the women staying there.

It's easy to be overwhelmed by the magnitude of need in the world, much of which we feel there is very little we can do about. Mother Teresa once pointed out, "It is easy to love the people far away. It is not always easy to love those close to us. It is easier to give a cup of rice to relieve hunger than to relieve the loneliness and pain of someone unloved in our own home. Bring love into your home for this is where our love for each other must start."[19] Bono's mother and father are largely unknown and yet he credits them for having supplied an example of pressing beyond religious differences for a higher good. In most cases, my family's efforts in alleviating the sufferings of the world occur right in our neighborhood and the people we meet or become aware of through daily life and interactions. Jessica is involved alongside us, and it may be that our greatest gift to a world in need will be our daughter, Jessica, and how we have invested our lives in her as parents.

We are continuously reminded there is deep hate and catastrophic suffering in our world. CNN presents a global smorgasbord of it 24/7 for us all to see. I am more aware of hate and suffering in my own community and city, and I have learned through several years in inner-city ministry that people who hate and afflict others are usually broken and hurting people themselves. Jesus taught not to repay evil with evil, and I'm finding that namaste is a practical way of living this.

In my mind's eye I can see a man who harbors resentment toward me because I am attached to a label that he

---

19. Mother Teresa, *Big Wisdom (Little Book): 1,001 Proverbs, Adages, and Precepts to Help You Live a Better Life,* (Nashville: Thomas Nelson Publishers, 2005), 101.

believes represents everything he is against in the world. I'm imagining coming upon the man along the paths of life and feeling his bitterness. I carry God's love for that man and the whole world within me, and so I will say to him, "Sir, sixty-five hundred Africans die every day of a preventable, treatable disease, for lack of drugs you and I can buy at any drugstore. One million girls every year around the world are forced into child prostitution because the will to stop it pales in comparison to the will to perpetuate it. Every day one hundred thousand American children are homeless. Right now in Nashville, fifteen families with small children live in their cars. If you don't tell me your religious beliefs, I won't tell you mine. Right now I humbly greet and honor you in that place where you and I are one, that place of God's love for the 'least of these.'"

Namaste.

chapter eight

Spiritual Living
Do We Need a Purpose in Life to Live?

A large, white possum finds something to eat next to the fence that runs along the trail I frequent. Using the entirety of my knowledge concerning sneaking up on something in the woods, most of which I acquired watching the late, great "Crocodile Hunter" Steve Irwin, I stealthily approach the possum fully absorbed in a feast of walnuts and black raspberries. As I get closer, a stick I didn't see under that pretty red maple leaf snaps beneath my feet. The possum is suddenly silent or in PSM (possum stealth mode). Not a breath of movement from him, just a big lump of white. Clever. He's playing dead. It's an odd tactic but a way of protecting himself nonetheless. After observing him quietly from the path for a few moments, I trek on.

On another pathway we frequent regularly on our family walks, it's not out of the ordinary to spot a caterpillar slowly inching across the pavement. Jessica and I saw one and stooped down to check it out. Jessica asked what would happen if she touched it. I said, "Let's see," and she gently reached down with her finger and touched the caterpillar's back. It responded by quickly forming itself into a ball. No amount of coaxing caused it to unfold, and it showed no sign of life. Once again, playing dead.

I've been on a spiritual path of sorts, the journey of discovering all of who I am and what that means. In my heart I come upon places where fears and old wounds keep me from being fully alive to all of life. I'm pretty good at playing dead myself, when things get too close to sensitive areas. For the possum and caterpillar, playing dead is a temporary measure; but I've discovered it's not wise to keep playing dead as a way of dealing with difficult issues. Living requires vulnerability, which is not possible while hiding out in the refuge of an overly protected self. Parts of me are just now, at forty-one, waking up and coming alive. As more of me comes alive, I realize too much of me is still playing dead.

For many years I assumed finding my "purpose" was the secret to a meaningful and fulfilling life. It was just one of those universally accepted facts that each of us is born to do something, and life is incomplete until you determine what that "something" is and do it. My childhood was one of drifting purposelessly through time. I wasn't involved in extracurricular happenings at school and never really developed a main interest, passion, or hobby. As I got older, it troubled me more because I saw other guys excel in sports, music, and mechanics. As time went on, I became more intent on finding some (any) purpose. I reasoned it out as follows:

   a. Everyone is born to do something.
   b. Whatever that something is, you will be wildly suc-
      cessful at it because, if you were born to do it, you are
      especially gifted and skilled to excel in it.
   c. Being wildly successful at something makes you some-
      body and people take notice and applaud accordingly.

I was desperate for some applause or a pat on the back,
for someone to notice me and affirm I had done something
good.

It was a great theory, but there was one little problem. I
wasn't overly intelligent, artistic, athletic, mechanically inclined,
or business oriented, and I couldn't rely on my looks. In short,
I couldn't do anything. What I had always hoped to be was
a professional basketball player or rock star. This may explain
why I've had a lifelong fascination with Michael Jordan and
Bono. Unfortunately, my vertical leap is measured by inches
instead of feet, and whenever I sing karaoke, I'm usually the
hit of the evening . . . because, as we know from *American
Idol*, sometimes the worst singer is the funniest. After failing
my junior year of high school, I eventually graduated and
squeaked into college. My decision to major in communica-
tions came down to, well, enjoying talking. In college my
desire to know God grew, and I found affirmation and acceptance in a Christian campus ministry. In my communication
classes I developed the skill for and became comfortable
with public speaking, and my faith drew me toward helping
people.

I vividly remember the outcome of my first gifting and
vocational assessment. The top three were:

1. Mortician
2. Politician
3. Pastor

I'm sure there's some hidden message in grouping these three together. "What do you have when you cross a mortician, politician, and pastor?" ME! At the time I wasn't laughing. Mortician? Are you kidding me? As I mentioned in a previous chapter, I'm easily spooked. Besides, I couldn't see picking up my date or driving the guys to the gym in a hearse, which is what would have happened since starting my Plymouth Horizon usually involved three Hail Mary's and two Our Father's. I did briefly flirt with becoming a politician, but dismissed it quickly after finding out the career path typically involved a law degree. I remembered the torture of a college class called "business law," which I had to take as part of my general education. If I had to learn a bunch of laws and stuff to be in government, forget it!

On the other hand, the decision to pursue the "pastor" path made complete sense. I genuinely desired to serve people and was gifted as a speaker and teacher. I was a leader in our campus ministry and the writing on the wall said, *Pastor Jim*. I pursued this path but unfortunately plugged my "calling" into the formula of becoming a somebody by doing something wildly successful. In the ministry, *wildly successful* meant leading a large church. If you could start a church from scratch and supersize it, you hit the applause jackpot. I was going to be a rock star one way or another!

Essentially the monster swallowed me whole. I built a growing ministry, but I was never satisfied with the size of results. There was always someone else in the spotlight who accomplished more for God than I did. Whenever I achieved another level of somebody status, more work and stress came along for the ride. I could never be satisfied or rest in my victories. It took tremendous energy, self-discipline, and commitment to maintain, protect, and add to my ministry achievements, all the while fearing I might fail.

Sometimes spiritual growth sneaks up on you. A twig snaps, and rather than play dead, you wake up and walk right through your greatest fear. In a recent interview I was asked, "What has been the most surprising thing to develop or happen directly because of your writing?" I began my reply by rattling off several things that came to mind in terms of opportunities I've had, places I've been, and people I've met as a result of writing *Divine Nobodies*. Then I said, "However, I'd have to say the most surprising thing is that writing has not stimulated a desire to be a somebody. Freedom is not needing or wanting to be anyone or anything more than who God says I am." Saying these words surprised me. So much of my life, I strived and strained to become someone important. Now as I was experiencing God's unconditional love and acceptance, my desire to fashion some important human identity diminished.

Somewhere back on my spiritual journey, there's a hill where I firmly planted in the ground a flag that reads: GOD IS ENOUGH. It is my flag of freedom, and it includes being liberated from the need to have a purpose. Notice I said *a* purpose. There is a big difference between determining some specific area of endeavor and excelling in it to feel good about yourself, and what it means to live out our eternal purpose here on earth.

In the Genesis garden, the picture of humankind is one

of peace and contentment with God, not of striving to find or add anything. Adam and Eve were not wandering around the garden fretting over what they were supposed to be doing for the rest of their lives; they simply enjoyed and rested in knowing God. My drive for determining *a* purpose in life was much ado about nothing. The apostle Paul identifies our purpose in the book of Philippians: "For my determined purpose is that I may know Him [that I may progressively become more deeply and intimately acquainted with Him, perceiving and recognizing and understanding the wonders of His person more strongly and more clearly]" (3:10 AMP).

Purpose is not something you *have*—a specific skill, gift, interest, passion, endeavor, vocation, volunteer involvement, or whatever. Instead, your existence is one unifying purpose, and every facet of your life is part of it. That unifying purpose is this: knowing God.

The Abbey of Gethsemani is a monastery in Trappist, Kentucky. I go once a year or so to enjoy an extended time of silence, solitude, and reflection. With Swiss precision, every morning at 5:15 the monks are praying in the abbey church. Likewise, at 5:15 every morning, Marjorie, who works in the kitchen, is mopping the floor. The monks and Marjorie have the same purpose and equal capacity and opportunity for fulfilling it. The monks are fulfilling that one purpose at 5:15 a.m. by praying. Marjorie is fulfilling that one and same purpose at 5:15 a.m. by mopping. It's possible Marjorie is more in tune with that one purpose than one of those monks. Maybe that particular monk was praying and singing solely out of obligation and routine with no sense of personal connection with God, while Marjorie was abiding in God's love and joy with each stoke of her mop.

During my stay at the abbey, I met a woman who enjoys photography. She said to me, "I meet God at the end of my lens." She uses the lens of her camera as a reminder to become "more deeply and intimately acquainted with Him." Her love for God is expressed as her love for photography. I hope you feel the freedom in that. God's purpose is not fulfilled by doing a lot of religious things you may or may not want to do. The things you love doing, what you are most passionate about, are the most significant avenues through which God wants you to know him. You have a love for these things because God placed it within you. David wrote in Psalm 37:4, "Delight yourself in the LORD and he will give you the desires of your heart." In other words, as you experience the joy and satisfaction of knowing God, follow your desires because God will be in them.

My focus on finding "a purpose" was a diversion that kept me so preoccupied both internally and externally, I missed the joy and adventure of simply knowing God. It's ironic the most profound ways of experiencing the reality of God are so utterly basic and part of everyday life. This may be why Jesus emphasized the need to become like a little child (Matthew 18:2–3). Adults complicate things; children keep it simple.

God's purpose for me, for you, for everyone is to know him. Knowing him satisfies and fulfills my deepest needs and desires and will for you too. In accepting this purpose, I've discovered a most astonishing fact about my human journey: God has rigged the world to conspire in my favor. His entire design for our earthly experience is designed to stimulate our knowing him. Everything God is (perfect love, peace, joy, freedom), he continually offers for us to experience. Opportunity abounds.

Pam, Jessie, and I took a few days to vacation at Land Between the Lakes in southern Kentucky. I was the first one up in the mornings and strolled down to the water's edge, where there was a bench. I sat looking out at Kentucky Lake, an enormous 170,000-acre body of water. You'd think you were staring out at the ocean if you didn't know better. Have you ever noticed how a body of water connects with something within you? It never fails that if I quiet myself and become observant around a lake, stream, or pond, a sense of wonder grows within, resulting in a deep sense of peace.

Looking out over the shimmering lake, a Scripture from Psalm 42 came to mind: "Deep calls to deep in the roar of your waterfalls; all your waves and breakers have swept over me" (v. 7). Suddenly my imagination was caught up in the mystery of the waters—its depths, its freedom of flow, its beauty and majesty, its gentleness, its power. I feel joy and freedom on the rise. The kingdom of God is flowing through my veins. Waves of divine love sweep over me. God had supplied this lake as a stimulus to know and experience him.

There's a lake not far from where we live. In fact, you have to drive over the dam to get to my neighborhood. I can't tell you how many times I've driven by that lake and given the water no attention. Why? Knowing God is simple, even if you're not off chasing after love and worth. There are times when life rains a zillion details, and instead of letting them roll off our back we act like a sponge and become so absorbed in them we miss most everything and everyone. In the busyness of life, I often close down.

That's why I become more aware of God on vacations and spiritual retreats. In those situations, I've left the zillion details behind and it's like I have a new pair of eyes. In this

openness I begin to see as God sees, viewing people, crea-
tures, and nature differently. As I open up and become more
aware, something happens inside me. The barriers of my
inattentiveness, judgments, or busyness move aside and allow
me to be in the moment 100 percent, connecting and bond-
ing with what's before me. At home, the tree in my front
yard is just a large object obstructing my view, which creates
a lot of work like raking leaves in the fall and spreading
mulch in the summer. At the abbey the trees seem to be the
splendor of God. What's the difference? God rigged the
world in our favor, but we still risk missing him if we are not
consciously aware of and receiving his presence. Or, as
Maltbie Babcock wrote, "Life is measured by the number of
things you are alive to."[20]

Living in God's rigged world requires our conscious
awareness. God often reaches out to us in simple ways, and
the marvels of who he is are often hiding in very ordinary
and inconspicuous things. I'm finding if I give attention to
whomever or whatever pops up along the paths of daily life,
they become an aspect of knowing God. Sometimes these are
moments of awareness like my Kentucky lake experience.
Normally they are simply day-to-day moments. The other
evening while strolling around the neighborhood with Jessica,
she took hold of my hand. It made me feel loved. As we continued walking hand in hand, I allowed myself to be fully in
that moment of experiencing my daughter's love. I realized I
wasn't just feeling Jessica's love but God's love in Jessica
for me.

---

20. Maltbie Babcock, *Thoughts for Every-day Living: From the Spoken and
    Written Words* (New York: Scribner, 1902), 84.

I've found I regularly experience the reality of God in my encounters and experiences of others. I close my eyes, and the faces of people I've met pass by me. Sometimes before going off to sleep at night I will intentionally think back through my day in order to remember the people I came across or interacted with. People continually come into my life at just the right moment. Some come to teach, others to comfort, some to challenge, and some to affirm. Some people offer me help when I am struggling, some give direction when I am searching, and others wake me when I'm lost in the endless barrage of yellow sticky notes. At times they are close friends, and at times they are complete strangers. People have brought me joy and gratitude, challenged my beliefs and attitudes, stretched me toward growth, and strengthened me by their presence.

I don't want to play dead in a world that God wired to help me fulfill my purpose of knowing him. My next e-mail or phone call, the next person I encounter, the next place I go, the next set of circumstances in my life, what I see outside my living room window or rearview mirror, the next words spoken, the next song on the radio . . . are all part of my life purpose of knowing God.

This learn-as-you-go way of relating to God wasn't always the case for me. In my twenty years of formal education, the process of learning was highly standardized and systematic. In college, my field of study was divided into independent subjects, in which large quantities of information were further broken down into categories and subcategories for easy digestion and memorization. At seminary, I organized God into theological categories such as Christology, soteriology, pneumatology, ecclesiology, missiology, and eschatology. I also learned to convert any portion of Scripture into a three-point sermon. It didn't matter if my text was one verse or twenty-one, some way or another it was going to end up as three points—perhaps fifteen subpoints, but three main points.

After completing my schooling, I began applying this orderly structure to life. For instance, I divided my existence into two main categories: "sacred" (God stuff) and "secular" (worldly stuff). At other times the breakdown was more elaborate, including categories such as: God and spiritual life, family life and leisure, vocation and personal finances, and diet and exercise. There was also a system I used for classifying people: Republican or Democrat, Christian or Muslim, American or Asian, SEC fan or Big Ten fan. I even once assigned the "fruit of the spirit" in Galatians 5:22–23 to a day of the week—my focus on Monday was love, Tuesday was joy, Wednesday was peace, and so on. God forbid I experience joy on Friday!

It wasn't easy getting out of my head that God isn't something you approach like a biology class. For years of my spiritual journey, God was a subject I split up into categories for mental consumption, a philosophy of life I applied through steps and principles, and a belief system I summarized in a creed. Outside the systematic mentality of religion, I discovered God is more like a dance partner in a Lindy Hop, the original swing dance.

In a Lindy Hop, an exhilarating and satisfying synergy grows with each spontaneous and improvisational step. Likewise, these last few years I have not set out to learn anything about God. In fact, I can't think of one class or group study I have attended about a specific subject related to God. It's more like my entire human existence is the classroom or

dance floor, and my spiritual growth unfolds out of an endless number of improvisational interactions with God and
the world around me.

The farther along I go with God, the more life feels like
a unified reality where everything is interrelated. Paul writes
in Romans 11:36, "For all things originate with Him and
come from Him; all things live through Him, and all things
center in and tend to consummate and to end in Him" (AMP).
Paul makes a similar point in a message recorded in Acts 17.
He begins by saying God made the world and everything in
it. Then he applies this truth to daily living: "Starting from
scratch, he made the entire human race and made the earth
hospitable, with plenty of time and space for living so we
could seek after God, and not just grope around in the dark
but actually *find* him. He doesn't play hide-and-seek with us.
He's not remote; he's near. We live and move in him, can't
get away from him!" (vv. 26–28 MSG).

I have found Paul's words to be true. God is always there
and I am as close to God as a fish is to the ocean. My life in
God is not a bunch of separate and independent areas or
subjects; there is a divine flow to all things.

It saddens me to ponder the possibility that out of all the
millions of believers in God, perhaps only a relatively few
make God a reality. If God *is* love, *is* joy, *is* peace, *is* life,
what would our lives be like if we were continuously aware
this God is always there and everywhere? Yes, God's presence is within me, with every sense I perceive God in the
world as I go about my day. I see him at the end of the lens
of my eye. I hear his voice in the words of others. I feel his
presence along the path of swaying trees. In the woods and
in the crowd, there is God.

Maybe this is what Paul meant when he wrote, "So here's what I want you to do, God helping you: Take your every-day, ordinary life—your sleeping, eating, going-to-work, and walking-around life—and place it before God as an offering. Embracing what God does for you is the best thing you can do for him" (Romans 12:1 MSG).

The worship or "offering" God desires from us is "embracing what God does for us" in our everyday lives. What does God do for us? He is continually stimulating our awareness of him through nature, friendship, parenting, music, silence, film, Scripture, work, and the tasks of daily living. God wants us to find him in it all.

This is spiritual living: everything and everyone a part of knowing God.

chapter nine

Follow the White Rabbit
Is God Slipping Messages to Humankind
Through Netflix?

M ORPHEUS. *I imagine that right now, you're feeling a bit like Alice. Hm? Tumbling down the rabbit hole?*

NEO. *You could say that.*

MORPHEUS. *I see it in your eyes. You have the look of a man who accepts what he sees because he is expecting to wake up. Ironically, that's not far from the truth. Do you believe in fate, Neo?*

NEO. *No.*

MORPHEUS. *Why not?*

NEO. *Because I don't like the idea that I'm not in control of my life.*

MORPHEUS. *I know exactly what you mean. Let me tell you why you're here. You're here because you know something. What you know you can't explain, but you feel it. You've felt it your entire life, that there's something wrong with the world. You don't know what it is, but it's there, like a splinter in your mind, driving you mad. It is this feeling that has brought you to me. Do you know what I'm talking about?*

NEO. *The Matrix.*

MORPHEUS. *Do you want to know what it is?*

NEO. *Yes.*

MORPHEUS. *The Matrix is everywhere. It is all around us. Even now, in this very room. You can see it when you look out your window or when you turn on your television. You can feel it when you go to work . . . when you go to church . . . when you pay your taxes. It is the world that has been pulled over your eyes to blind you from the truth.*

NEO. *What truth?*

MORPHEUS. *That you are a slave, Neo. Like everyone else you were born into bondage. Into a prison that you cannot taste or see or touch. A prison for your mind. I'm trying to free your mind, Neo. But I can only show you the door. You're the one that has to walk through it.*

NEO. *Why do my eyes hurt?*

MORPHEUS. *You've never used them before. Neo, sooner or later you're going to realize just as I did that there's a difference between knowing the path and walking the path. Have you ever had a dream, Neo, that you were so sure was real? What if you were unable to wake from that dream? How would you know the difference between the dream world and the real world? Welcome to the real world.*

God used the film *The Matrix* to help awaken me spiritually. The story deeply connected with a truth I felt in the core of my being for some time: there are two worlds. From time to time during my journey through religion, I heard this voice inside saying there was something more than what I was experiencing—more to life, more to God, more to faith, more to existence. Most of the time I ignored the voice, doubted the voice, and was too concerned over what people would think of me to risk asking others if they heard it too. But I couldn't shut the voice up. I went to church, read my Bible, and did things good Christians do, but there was still this nagging sense in my gut that there was much more to it than that. As Morpheus told Neo, it was "like a splinter in your mind."

Essentially *The Matrix* prepared me for the spiritual bomb Jesus dropped into my life. It detonated one night while I was comfortably sprawled out on our living room couch. Pam, Jessie, and I were enjoying our evening, all comfy in the living room chatting about our journeys with God— ways we experience God, questions we were pondering, or some situation or need we felt compelled to become involved in or seek wisdom about in prayer. One particular night, Pam read a portion of Scripture. Easter was approaching, which drew her to the Gospel accounts of Jesus' last few days on earth. One night, she read John 18:33–38 (NASB), where Pilate questions Jesus before handing him over to be crucified.

The exchange goes as follows:

> PILATE. *Are you the King of the Jews?*
> JESUS. *My kingdom is not of this world. If My*

*kingdom were of this world, then My servants would
be fighting so that I would not be handed over to the
Jews; but as it is, My kingdom is not of this realm.*

PILATE. *So You are a king?*

JESUS. *You say correctly that I am a king. For this
I have been born, and for this I have come into the
world, to testify to the truth. Everyone who is of the
truth hears My voice.*

PILATE. *What is truth?*

After Pam read these words, time stood still and everything else was tuned out, while Jesus' words reverberated in my head: "My kingdom is not of this world . . . not of this world . . . not of this world . . . My kingdom is not of this realm . . . not of this realm . . . not of this realm." Sure I had read that passage before and probably preached a few sermons on it, but apparently it went in one ear and out my mouth without taking up residence. But in that moment on the couch, a staggering realization and unsettling question swept over me:

Realization: There are indeed two worlds.
Question: Which one am I living in?

Jesus' claim that his kingdom was not of this world or realm consumed me. I was determined to understand the reality and meaning of what he said. The next morning I woke up, got out of bed, put in my contacts, and started brewing a pot of coffee. Then I walked out on our back deck to check the weather and was rudely reminded of needing to mow our lawn. This wasn't going to be easy, since moles turned our entire backyard into something resembling a battle-field. I would be mowing dirt mounds. Right around the time I began having *Caddyshack* thoughts about the moles, it hit me. I live in a physical, material world—a world of coffeepots, lawnmowers, and moles. This material world is the reality I am most conscious of because I experience life through my five physical senses. I engage, evaluate, and judge in accordance to what I hear, see, smell, touch, and taste.

Jesus, on the other hand, said his kingdom was not of this physical, material world. When Pilate asked Jesus if he was a king, Pilate was thinking of a material and political king with earthly power. Jesus responded by saying if his was such a kingdom, he would have simply sent his follow-ers to wage war, which is typically how such kingdoms are established.

This isn't the only place Jesus described the spiritual nature of his kingdom. In another encounter, Jesus is asked when the kingdom of God would drop down out of the sky and what it would look like. Astonishingly, Jesus replied the kingdom of God had already come and could be experienced within and among them. You can imagine the resulting blank stares as people struggled to imagine a kingdom we experi-ence right now through means other than the five physical senses. But we know it must exist because as Helen Keller said, "The most beautiful things in the world cannot be seen or touched; they must be felt with your heart."[21]

During his exchange with Pilate, Jesus gives an explana-

---

21. Helen Keller, *Big Wisdom (Little Book): 1,001 Proverbs, Adages, and Precepts to Help You Live a Better Life*, (Nashville: Thomas Nelson Publishers, 2005), 200.

tion of his purpose: "For this I have come into the world, to testify to the truth." What truth? The truth of what lies beyond the physical, material world, namely a spiritual world, realm, or kingdom. It's a spiritual reality we engage through spiritual awareness. Paul referred to such awareness when he wrote, "So we fix our eyes not on what is seen, but on what is unseen. For what is seen is temporary, but what is unseen is eternal" (2 Corinthians 4:18). Physical eyes see a material world, but Paul prayed that the "eyes of your heart may be enlightened" (Ephesians 1:18). Morpheus put it this way: "I'm trying to free your mind."

I soon realized that when Jesus said, "Seek first my kingdom," he essentially said, "Don't be absorbed by your material world. Seek the invisible, spiritual reality behind it." At first this conjured up images of some bald, robed guru in a desert or on a mountaintop chanting and groaning unintelligibly in some hypnotic state while assuming the flying grasshopper. I was in trouble. I would look terrible bald, and being in one position for any length of time kills my back.

Thankfully, common sense ousted the images and idea of the robed guru. Jesus did seek out times of silence, solitude, and meditation, but he didn't sit on mountaintops in hypnotic states. In fact, Jesus seemed fully engaged in the world of coffeepots, lawnmowers, and moles. He encountered the realities of life as any first-century Jew. Yet everyone could see that something about Jesus was decidedly different. Though Jesus lived in the material world, he approached it and engaged it from a spiritual consciousness. Jesus explained his way of living by saying he was *in* the world but not *of* the world. He experienced life through spiritual discernment, with his physical words and actions guided by the spiritual world's realities.

I understood in a new way what Jesus meant when he said, "I am the way and the truth and the life" (John 14:6). Jesus was saying he was the demonstration of the truth—God's physical creation functioning as one with God, the perfect fusion of the physical and spiritual. Jesus was the perfect unity of both worlds—fully God, fully human, one reality. The rabbit hole was getting deeper and deeper.

Jesus baited humankind by instructing people to pray for God's kingdom to unfold "on earth as it is in heaven" (Matthew 6:10). Jesus would not say this if he thought it impossible. Let me ask you: Is it believable a loving God would place life, beauty, and freedom in our hearts only to place us in our world full of emptiness, bondage, and despair or at best conditional love and peace? Is it believable a loving God would want humankind waging war against one another as means of living in safety, security, and peace? Would any soldier say he (or she) actually *wanted* to go to war? Usually soldiers and their family and friends are the first to celebrate when conflict is resolved peacefully.

There is no shortage of evidence that people and creation function in disrepair and suffering when living in the world *and* of the world, unaided by the spiritual dimension. Yet the radical message of Jesus is that the spiritual world and material world can function as one unified reality. When I realized this, I wondered, *Is this really possible? Can God's spiritual kingdom of perfect love, truth, peace, beauty, joy, and freedom be the right-now, living reality of this physical human world? Can both worlds exist at the same time?* Jesus answered pretty decisively: "All things are possible with God" (Matthew 19:26).

In some ways, this is an inconvenient truth. I would rather

engross myself in temporal pleasures of the material world, maybe add a little religion here and there, but essentially wait for God to wave his magic wand and fix all the problems or snap his fingers and magically download the new world himself. The idea that the suffering and hardship of this human existence isn't necessary seems to put a big burden on my shoulders that, frankly, I don't want or know what to do with.

Jesus' disciples were once confronted with an overwhelming situation as thousands of hungry people were gathered together without a nearby McDonald's to grab a bite to eat. The disciples approached Jesus and asked him to wave his magic God-wand and fix it. Jesus essentially replied, "No, you fix it." In the end the solution was a collaborative effort, Jesus and his disciples acting as one. Jesus was illustrating the distinction between "all things are possible" and "all things are possible *with God*."

The truth is, we are already halfway there. God's spiritual kingdom already exists within you. You've caught glimpses of it. You can't explain why or what caused it. Driving in your car, standing in line, hiking through the woods, sitting in a movie, watching your kid's soccer game, talking with a friend, the voice of God through Scripture, you felt it. Time stood still and you were seized in a moment of bliss where you felt perfectly loved, completely free, at peace, and one with all things. You smiled. Maybe you looked around to see if anyone noticed. Perhaps you even questioned your sanity. Whatever it was, it was well with your soul.

You experienced the reality of God in the depths of your being. You stepped into the kingdom of God! Perhaps you mistakenly attributed it to a breathtaking sunrise, captivating film, or your bike or boat wide-open throttle against the wind. But you felt it only because it is already in you. Any truly good feeling you have ever felt is because the source, the presence of God, is within you. Sometimes a gentle summer breeze or faint train whistle in the night mysteriously makes you aware of it.

In those moments it all comes together in a way that lets you know deep down that this is the "more" you always knew there was. It's not what television commercials are telling you, not what you see with your eyes or touch with your hands or have in your checking account, it may not even be what you hear in church on Sunday. But you know that you know when it floods into your soul and you feel loved, free, at peace, full of joy, and wonderfully part of a greater whole, that this is the most real and solid world there is. It's the same world where people don't sleep in cardboard boxes on city streets, or kill someone for a pair of Nike basketball shoes, or hate others because of the color of their skin. It's all in you. Perhaps now it exists only as a tiny seed in terms of your daily experience, but as Jesus pointed out, that's the way the kingdom of God goes. It begins as the smallest seed and becomes the largest tree.

I've stepped into this kingdom myself, but years of religious programming stopped me from going with it for a while. I learned to mistrust and invalidate what I most deeply felt within. Instead, it was impressed upon me to have the right belief system and be done with it. Fear kept me in my head where God is known on paper, captured in creeds, and mediated through the goods, services, and personalities of Christendom; reasonable, safe, and doable. You can abandon it in fear, bury it beneath religion, lose it amid the glitz and glimmer of earthly things, even pass it off as a beautiful autumn day or extraordinary piece of music, but the kingdom of God within you cannot be fully suppressed. If nothing else, it will taunt you as a splinter in your mind.

What you felt in those moments of bliss is the kingdom of God emanating from the source or King within you. If you allow yourself to live and speak from that inner reality, you will give birth to the kingdom of God around you and shape a new world. It's really only a "new" world because much of our present reality is a false world. The real world is God and his perfect love, perfect peace, perfect joy, perfect unity, perfect goodness, and perfect freedom. The absence of these things is a false world. Morpheus referred to it as "the matrix." This false reality is passing away. You can help it along by living what's real.

Consider light. At first glance, light and dark seem to be opposites. But they're not, really. Light is the presence of a certain type of energy, and darkness is the absence of light. Darkness only exists when the flow of light energy is blocked or obstructed by something. You can't make "darkbulbs," "flashdarks," or flip on a "darkswitch" to make darkness, because darkness is not something you can make. That is to say, darkness is only a shadow, a place where the light has not reached. Rather than having opposites, what we actually have is simply the presence of some quality (light), or the absence of that quality (darkness).

The kingdom of God is the only true reality, but people do choose to live in the absence of that reality. Hate, greed, injustice, lust, and desperate striving for peace, purpose, meaning, worth, and happiness exists because the reality of God is being blocked or obstructed. We have eyes to see but do not see. Sometimes we open our eyes, letting the reality of the kingdom of God reach our consciousness, and sometimes we close our eyes because we're comfortable in the darkness. We are living in the world with our eyes closed, or opening and closing our eyes depending on the situation or circumstance.

If there were no war, hunger, crime (because there is no evil) or need to find meaning, worth, and love (because we have everything we need), what would we be free to do or become? This is not a rhetorical question about some far-off and distant possibility. The question lies before you in this very moment, and you can live your way into the answer now. You have already experienced the spiritual qualities of God's kingdom within you. But that doesn't go far enough. Our longing and destiny is to, as Paul writes, "shine like stars in the universe" by being all these things (Philippians 2:15). Me, you, us: being love, being goodness, being beauty, being freedom, being joy, being forgiveness, being compassion, being one with God.

So, you ask, what do I do? Hmm . . . *do*? Well, here's something that comes to mind. Next time you are seized in a divine moment when you connect fully with some attribute(s) of the kingdom of God, don't rush past it or pass it off as some sappy warm fuzzy. Stop and let yourself soak it in until it begins dripping and running off you. What is the feeling? What kind of thoughts is this feeling producing in your heart and mind about you, about God, about life? What would it mean to go with these thoughts and feelings and allow them to direct the way you go about your day, your motivation behind what you do, the way you relate to people? The most transformational experiences of our lives result from living out and experiencing the eternal realities of the kingdom of God. For instance, when we speak to someone out of the perfect love within us, they not only experience that attribute of God, but they are also freed to speak and live out of the kingdom of God within themselves.

Recently I experienced the perfect love of God within me, and it spawned the realization that this perfect love goes with me into my day and world. It was big enough for me to offer it as a free gift in some way to every person with whom I cross paths.

As we recognize the stirrings of God inside, we begin to live in a conscious (right now) awareness of God's presence and kingdom within us. As this becomes our new spiritual atmosphere, the new world begins to unfold and we see Jesus' prayer, "Your kingdom come . . . on earth as it is in heaven," become a present reality (Matthew 6:10). What is true of the spiritual kingdom within expresses and manifests itself in the visible experiences of our earthly lives.

I have a lot of friends who believe a lot of different things about God. From time to time, I'm asked why I place so much significance on Jesus. I recently responded by saying Jesus is my "Morpheus," the one who opens the eyes of my heart to the spiritual world and shows me what it means to live in it. The truth of Jesus is the red pill. Jesus' claim that his kingdom was not of this world or realm became the "rabbit hole" I tumbled down. When I hit bottom, Jesus was standing there and said, "Welcome, Jim, to the real world."

There seems to be this pattern emerging in my journey with God and how I'm growing spiritually. It goes something like this:

Pattern: Something stimulates my desire to seek and
know truth.
Example: The film *The Matrix*[22]

Pattern: My desire is rewarded and my spiritual eyes
are opened to truth.
Example: There are two worlds God desires to function
as one.

Pattern: The new truth sets me free.
Example: I can live in oneness with and birth his
kingdom into the world around me.

Pattern: My desire for truth intensifies.
Example: I seek truth more earnestly and the process
begins again.

The net result of this pattern is a deepening desire and
love for truth. There are times when my love for truth causes
me to let go of certain aspects of my religious tradition. It
also greatly influences the way I think of and relate to people.
People are an image or reflection of God, regardless of their
religious tradition or spiritual beliefs. Many have discovered
something of the truth I have yet to encounter or uncover. As
I relate to others, I'm thinking, *This person knows something I don't and I want to be open to learning it.* Simply said,
we are all students and teachers.

---

22. God used many movies to get me started down some path I needed to
travel. God has used the creative genius of M. Night Shyamalan many
times in my spiritual journey. Apparently, God has been slipping messages to humankind through Netflix.

Pam, Jessie, and I recently helped cook and serve dinner for parents currently staying at the Nashville Ronald McDonald House, which provides a home away from home for families of seriously ill children receiving treatment at nearby hospitals. A couple of children with cancer also joined us for the meal. In the kitchen on the door is a whiteboard, on which is a list of the various people or groups providing the evening meals for the week. There's no way of knowing the specifics of these volunteers, such as their age, vocation, or religious beliefs. All I knew from the board is they volunteered for a night to serve these families of terminally ill children.

What most moved me about the experience was seeing these moms and dads, complete strangers prior to meeting at the house, express love, care, and compassion for one another. They were some of the kindest and gentlest people I've ever met. It was humbling to see and be on the receiving end of their kindheartedness, given their hardship. I tried to put myself in their shoes and imagine if it were my Jessica without any hair and suffering through cancer treatments.

As I drove home I wondered what living in the present reality of God's kingdom could mean for these sick children and their parents. At a stoplight on Old Hickory Boulevard, it hit me: I had experienced what it meant. The volunteers who had prepared and served the meals, as well as the parents who received them, were all offering and receiving love. The hardship of their human circumstances did not hinder the spiritual reality of God's kingdom.

There are all kinds of places where a person can get a copy of my last book, *Divine Nobodies*. But wherever those places might be, I feel the greatest joy from knowing a copy is sitting on the bookcase at that Ronald McDonald House in Nashville. I placed it there that night after I signed it in honor of the children and their families. At some point, a hurting mom or dad will wander over to that bookshelf, wanting to lose themselves for a while in some diversion. I hope that person spots *Divine Nobodies*, pulls it out, and notices what I wrote inside along with my signature: "To all the parents at the Ronald McDonald House, thank you for showing me love and kindness. May the truth set you free."

Perhaps the person reading it will be perplexed to know that parents just like them were on the giving end, not the receiving end. Maybe this will create a "splinter" in the person's mind as he or she thinks, *How could someone like me, heartbroken with a terminally ill child, ever move beyond my hurt and fear to love strangers?*

Somewhere deep within, a person becomes aware of contact with another reality. Maybe this will be the time.

chapter ten

The Freedom Filter

Can We Trust Our Gut?

W e are simultaneously living our lives in two dimensions—a physical dimension and a spiritual dimension. Both dimensions contain truth, but they are different kinds of truth. Truth in the physical dimension changes and is temporary, so it's *t*ruth with a little *t*. Truth in the spiritual dimension is unchanging, absolute, and permanent, so it's Truth with a capital *T*. It's not always easy separating these truths accordingly. For example, try these True/False questions:

True or False? Jim Palmer is Truth.

False. He can't be, because Jim Palmer changes and Truth doesn't change. Science says I'm not even the same person right now as I was two seconds ago when I wrote the above sentence. You aren't either.

True or False? You and I together are Truth.

False. The answer must be false for the same reason as above. No matter how many of us we stick together, each and every one of us is changing, and Truth does not change. The church is not Truth because the church is people and people change. No organization of humans is the Truth.

True or False? The world and all of nature is Truth.

False. The world and nature change. The Grand Canyon was once a desert plain until rain started falling, a river started flowing, and the persistence of the water wore down the resistance of the rock. Mount Saint Helens once had a peak, but on May 18, 1980, the peak was blown off of it in an eruption. The things of this world change.

True or False? The Bible on the table is Truth. (Is this a tricky one?)

False. Yep, false. Truth was Truth long before the Bible was written or printed. Something's not true because it's in the Bible; it's in the Bible because it's true. Adam didn't have a Bible, but he knew Truth.

Spiritual Truth never changes, but the forms that express spiritual Truth do. Spiritual Truth is expressed through the words of Scripture, but it is also expressed through people, music, film, and nature. The forms themselves are not Truth. Truth is not a *what* but a *who*. Truth is God himself. Truth is a spiritual reality, and it belongs to the spiritual realm.

Our physical dimension contains the little-*t* truth of this world, a mass of information and a collection of temporary facts. We encounter the truths of the physical dimension through our five senses. Many of these truths change depending on our environment, our circumstances, and us. For example, if you're standing in the middle of train tracks, they seem to come to a point out on the horizon, but from the sky we see they remain parallel. In that sense, truth is relative and depends on your perspective.

God gave every human the authority, power, and right to know what is true and what is false, what is good and what is bad, what is beautiful and what is downright ugly. God enables people to decide Truth by listening to his voice within them. So deciding what's true is an individual, personal judgment that comes from the heart or the God-life within us. The Scriptures say we know the Truth by the Spirit of Truth. So confirming Truth with physical data is a really bad move. Like the people who evaluated Jesus by physical data and surmised he was just a nice but poor carpenter and philosopher. God is Spirit. It is his Spirit within that makes him known to us. The real confirmation of Truth is God's Spirit setting us free in our spirits, telling us, *Yes, this is true; it brings freedom.*

Religion too often teaches people to depend on others for Truth. It's easy to understand how this happens. In the physical dimension, we are taught that the smartest, most educated people know more truth than we do. The scientist knows more truth about the universe. The doctor knows more truth about the human body. The lawyer knows more truth about the legal field. Our knowledge in these areas is miniscule compared to the knowledge of these professionals. They *really* know.

Religion applies this rationale to the spiritual realm and spiritual Truth. We come to assume that the people who know

God best are people with seminary educations and positions of Christian leadership. Let me show you.

If you need surgery, you go to a surgeon.

If you need legal advice, you go to a lawyer.

If you need a new alternator, you go to a mechanic.

If you need understanding about some spiritual matter, you go to _God_ ?

Do you go to your hairstylist, a UPS driver, or your garbage man? Well, maybe if your pastor is bivocational. No. You seek out a pastor, a Bible professor, someone who knows Greek and Hebrew—a person you perceive as highly knowledgeable about God. Perhaps you purchase the latest book written by the person you are confident has a deeper knowledge of spiritual things than you do. What if you picked up a book entitled *Knowing God* and the author's bio read, "Fred Brown never completed high school. He cleans fish on the docks of Daytona Beach. He lives with his two monkeys, three ducks, and one ferret in a camper"? Would you buy it?

The idea is that a "professional minister" has a better functioning spirit with which to discern Truth than you have. So, let me ask you, can higher education further develop and improve upon the Spirit's capacity to discern Truth? Why do some of the most highly educated people in the world think there is no absolute or big-*T* Truth, and consider the Bible nothing more than fabrication and fairy tales? On the other hand, some of the most spiritual people I know do not have formal Bible training or schooling of any kind beyond high school.

Many people like to know about things so they study and study, learn and learn, memorize facts and figures, and fill their head with all the knowledge on a certain topic. But we all realize there's a difference between "knowledge" and "knowing." For instance, Pam and I went to a marriage conference before we actually tied the knot. We thought it was a great idea to get a head start on learning what it meant to have a healthy and fulfilling husband-wife relationship. During the weeklong conference, we filled a thick fill-in-the-blank notebook covering topics such as accepting each other's differences and weaknesses, dealing with conflict, and the importance of communication.

This was all well and good, but there was one big problem. None of this information applied to us. How could I accept Pam's weaknesses? She didn't have any. Pam was perfect! Resolving conflict? What conflict? We *loved* each other. It was hard to imagine ever getting to a point where Pam and I would disagree or argue about anything. Why did I need someone telling me how to communicate with Pam? Our relationship was one continuous and euphoric flow of sharing our deepest thoughts and feelings.

Instead of paying attention to the speakers, we doodled little love notes to each other on our workbooks and referred to each other with endearing names like "Pumpkin" and "Birdy." Recently looking through our conference notebooks, I noticed one of the little notes that Pam wrote on mine says, "I radically love you." Hmm . . . brings to mind that line from that old Olivia Newton John song, "I ~~honestly~~ radically love you." Okay seriously, I don't really listen to Olivia Newton John . . . or Cher.

There are all sorts of things you don't truly "know," even if you've got all the correct information filled in the blanks. You can't accept your spouse's weaknesses until you discover there are some, or learn how to resolve conflicts until you start having them. Pam and I *know* what a fulfilling marriage is because we have experienced each other's human flaws, but we allow God's unconditional love and acceptance for us to spill over into loving and accepting each other. Sure, when we are operating out of our worldly selves, we sometimes wound each other with hurtful words and attitudes. But the fulfillment of living and sharing life as best friends supplies plenty of motivation to seek forgiveness and resolve conflicts so we can get back to what we both most enjoy—each other. Some things you can't truly know unless you experience them for yourself.

Too often we become dependent on other people—a favorite leader, teacher, speaker, author—for determining Truth. Rather, it's helpful to see those roles are really "sheepdog" roles. The sheepdog role is to get sheep (people) to the Shepherd (God). That's it. That's what I hope this book accomplishes in some way. I hope it points you into the direction of God, or connects you to the reality of God, or frees you to pursue God. Then your knowing and interacting with the presence of God within you takes over.

There is a sizable gap between the number of knowledgeable Christians and the number of Christians who express the reality of God. Why is that? Really, why is that? I wonder if it's because we too often take someone else's word for the Truth, rather than experiencing for ourselves God's Spirit confirming Truth within us. Maybe that's the difference between knowledge and knowing. We acquire knowledge by absorbing teachings others show us, but knowing occurs when the life of God within you reveals Truth and *your* spirit says, "I know that I know."

John wrote, "My dear friends, don't believe everything

you hear. Carefully weigh and examine what people tell you" (1 John 4:1 MSG). John understood that ultimately people must discern Truth for themselves. Someone else can share with you what God revealed to him (that's knowledge), but until God reveals it to you (that's knowing), all you have is knowledge of what God revealed to someone else. Sure, discerning Truth for yourself might seem like a pretty daunting proposition. But I've found God has supplied a simple means of discerning Truth. It's called the freedom filter.

Simply, I funnel potential Truth through the filter of freedom and follow only what leads to freedom. Paul wrote in Galatians 5:1: "Christ has set us free to live a free life. So take your stand! Never again let anyone put a harness of slavery on you" (MSG). Paul also said, "For where the Spirit of the Lord is, there is freedom" (2 Corinthians 3:17).

I am constantly exposed to claims of Truth. Sometimes these claims come from others—an author, a pastor, a teacher, or a friend expressed through a book, sermon, song, or statement. At other times, these claims of Truth come from my interpretation of Scripture, my observation of nature, or whatever I come up with as my mind interacts with what I am feeling inside. Whether it's coming from outside or inside, I am continuously confronted with claims of Truth. My freedom filter asks the following question about whatever Truth claim is before me: *Will this Truth bring freedom?* If my answer is yes, I accept the Truth as my Truth. If my answer is no—in other words, if believing or accepting this Truth leads to bondage or slavery—I say no and reject it.

Sometimes when I am depressed, my worldly self says eating something will make me feel better. So I escape my depressed feelings by doing the following: I get a large bowl and fill it with cookies-and-cream ice cream. I raid our candy stash and sprinkle whatever I can find on top, like M&Ms, gummy bears, or my absolute favorite, Jelly Belly's . . . somebody stop me. Sometimes we have a bag of chocolate morsels and that works too. Then I top it all off with a dollop (read: mountain) of Cool Whip and dive in. Of course, I wash it all down with a Diet Coke; gotta keep those calories down, right? It feels sooo good for a few moments, but then I'm left with a hangover of self-hatred and the burden of jogging an extra mile the next day. Temporarily anesthetizing my pain and emptiness with a super-tasty sugar high isn't exactly "freedom."

What I mean by "freedom" is doing what your spiritual self desires, *not* whatever your worldly self wants. Freedom is a way of living. It's being a willing slave to perfect love, unconditional acceptance, perfect peace, boundless joy, and the abundant life. Jesus expressed freedom in his sacrifice. Paul expressed freedom while singing in the gallows of jail. The disciples expressed freedom by dropping their nets in the midst of a day's work and following Christ. Mother Teresa expressed freedom through her life of serving others. Nelson Mandela expressed freedom by living in prison for twenty-seven years. Martin Luther King, Jr. expressed freedom by choosing to march in the face of death threats. And every single person reading these words expresses freedom in living for others. Freedom is not selfish but selfless; thinking of others is an expression of freedom. Freedom is part of the air we breathe in the kingdom of God.

Freedom involves liberation from one's misplaced dependencies; those things that are not God that we use to fill our need for unconditional love and acceptance, and purpose and meaning in life. A. W. Tozer describes it as "the blessedness of possessing nothing."[23] No job, person, endeavor, talent, thrill, formula, achievement, or amount of ice cream brings true life, worth, significance, peace, love, wholeness, and fulfillment. Only as we depend solely on the life of God within to satisfy our needs does striving give way to rest, complete rest. Depending on other things is like sitting on a hard wooden chair, while depending on God is like resting in the glovelike fit of your favorite recliner—your entire being is supported at every point.

Freedom filters out anything that pulls you away from these qualities or expressions of God. If a claim of Truth stimulates freedom resulting from God's grace and love, I go with it. But if some claim of Truth draws me into fear, negativity, worry, captivity, legalism, depression, dependency, hatred, or condemnation, I toss it out. I'm not interested in "going there" anymore. Been there, done that. Designed the T-shirt. More than a few times I've been around Christians promoting "Truths" that built cells of captivity rather than wide open spaces of freedom. Sadly, more than a few times I've also been around knowledgeable Christians where I could feel the discomfort growing within me as I listened to what they were espousing or asking of me. And it's not a good feeling. I felt that if I bought into what they were selling, it would lead to all those aforementioned negative things.

Jesus lived and breathed a freedom to love, not a freedom from hate and selfishness. His focus wasn't on being

23. A. W. Tozer, *The Pursuit of God* (Camp Hill, PA: Christian Publications, 1994), 21.

free from sin but being alive to love. I wonder if that's why all the "sinners" in the Gospels were drawn to Jesus. Just being in his presence and listening to his words stirred freedom and wholeness in the human soul. He came to set all people free.

Okay, let's practice using the freedom filter. I will throw out a Truth claim, and we'll test it. Here's one I've heard quite a few times over the years in church sermons. It wasn't always stated in these exact words, but the implication is the same nonetheless.

> You are a sinner. Sure, you're a sinner "saved by grace," but you are still a sinner, because you sin. Here, I'll prove it. Did you tell a lie, even a white lie, today, this week, or this month? Like I said, you are a sinner and therefore condemned by God. (For those of you who just snubbed your nose because you haven't told even a white lie in the last thirty days, well, that air of confidence you're feeling right now is self-righteousness and it is also a sin . . . crazy how that works, isn't it?)

Now, let's test this Truth claim with our freedom filter by asking our key question: "Will this Truth bring freedom?"

By accepting this claim, my identity is a member of the human race whose standing before God is determined by my behavior. If I accept this claim of Truth, I will . . .

- *Avoid intimacy with God.* I don't like being around someone who condemns me, not even a God who condemns me. Even if I'm "saved," why would I want to be intimate with a God who once detested me so thoroughly, who can only look on me or be around me only because he's really seeing me as someone else? Maybe instead, I'll just make sure I believe the right things about God. After all, I sure don't want to be wrong about God and risk falling out of favor. I'm already skating on thin ice as it is.

- *Focus on behavior and doing.* God hates sin, and the Bible identifies a long list of them. I'll focus on keeping the big ten and doing what good Christians do, like go to church, read my Bible, tithe, and do good deeds. I'll judge myself and others based on my list of dos and don'ts.

When I turn on my freedom filter, it flashes "ALERT: DO NOT ACCEPT THIS MESSAGE. TURN THE OTHER DIRECTION AND RUN FOR YOUR LIFE!"

That Truth claim is incredibly egocentric. My starting point with God is not me! My starting point with God is . . . well . . . God!

Apparently, sometimes folks don't make the connection that Genesis 1 (where God creates humankind) precedes Genesis 3 (where humankind turns away from God). Each of us has always existed in God's mind and is held there in his love. God says to Jeremiah, "Before I shaped you in the womb, I knew all about you" (Jeremiah 1:5 MSG). Likewise, in Ephesians 1:4–6, Paul writes, "Long before he laid down earth's foundations, he had us in mind, had settled on us as the focus of his love, to be made whole and holy by his love. Long, long ago he decided to adopt us into his family through Jesus Christ. (What pleasure he took in planning this!) He wanted us to enter into the celebration of his lavish gift-giving by the hand of his beloved Son" (MSG).

First and foremost, we are the beloved creations of God. Eventually our expressions of God's love took on physical form through our human birth. The Truth is God has always loved you and will never stop loving you. God did not send Jesus into the world to condemn the world (John 3:17), but to set it free. Paul points out that God's love was demonstrated in the fact that Christ came despite our fallen condition (Romans 5:8).

Your birth certificate does not identify who you are. The real Jim came out of God and carries his divine life within. Your birth certificate says quite a bit of stuff about your human identity. However, it fails to say anything about your spiritual identity. If spiritual Truth never changes, then once a sinner always a sinner. That's the problem with that Truth claim. It is true we "sin" (that is, fall short of God's perfect love, joy, peace, and freedom), but God doesn't identify us by our behavior; he identifies us through our relationship with him—we are children of God.

That faulty Truth claim also sets up a faulty and frustrating premise for Christian living. The whole "sinner becomes saint" theory prompts me to strive toward becoming something more than what I presently am. The real deal is, my perfection as an expression or reflection of God is an established spiritual Truth. I can rest in that reality and let it be expressed through me. So, my freedom filter says to that Truth claim, "Don't accept it." That claim compels me to avoid intimacy with God and focus on my behavior. Once again, I've been there and done that and burned that stinking T-shirt, along with all my commitment cards.

Let's try using the freedom filter in relationships. In a conversation with your spouse or close friend, a disagreement arises and your spouse or friend says something negative about you. You internalize the negative remark, prompting negative thoughts and feelings about yourself. Within just a few seconds, your internalized pain moves you to prepare your own negative statement about your friend in response. You think, *Two can play this game.*

Okay, let's turn on the freedom filter. Will firing back with your own negative statement bring freedom? Won't that just reinforce the negative feelings about yourself that you are already experiencing? Even worse, doesn't doing so drag you down into the behavior associated with that false identity? Whatever your friend may have said or however it made you feel about yourself, the truth of who you are is not what that person says and what you feel by internalizing it. Your identity is based in God. You were made in the image of perfect love. Responding as perfect love is an expression of who you really are. By responding in love, you are also reinforcing the truth of your friend's identity. Responding with your own negative statement sets in motion the same cycle for your friend— she hears, internalizes, and responds in kind out of her false self. The freedom filter says that going back and forth with negative remarks further enslaves both of you to the false self.

If you ignore the freedom filter, the conversation might look like this:

SUSAN. *Julie, you are so selfish! Do you ever think of anybody except yourself?!*

JULIE. *Well, well, isn't that the pot calling the kettle black! You are the most prideful and self-centered person I know!*

(They storm off in opposite directions.)

With the freedom filter on:

SUSAN. *Julie, you are so selfish! Do you ever think of anybody except yourself?!*
JULIE. *Susan, I can see you're upset. Frankly, what you just said was hurtful. However, I care about you and our friendship. Let's talk through this together. I'm not going to let this disagreement come between us.*
(They hug and talk things out.)

The next story actually happened to me, and it was interesting to see how I put my freedom filter to use. I ran into someone I hadn't seen in a while at the grocery store. I used to know this person through my involvement in organized church. As we were chitchatting in the coffee aisle, this person asked, "So where do you go to church now?" I responded, "These days, 'church' for my family is focusing on the day-to-day relationships with all in our lives. How about you? How are things at Cedar Creek?" As if he didn't even hear my question, he said with dismay, "You don't go to church anymore? Do you think it's a good thing to be a 'Lone Ranger' Christian? What about accountability and biblical teaching?"

Now the ball was in my court. It was my choice how I wanted to respond. I could have chosen to feel the fear, negativity, and worry that his statements were created to produce, but instead, I asked myself, "If I accept what this person is telling me, will it lead to freedom? Do I feel the grace and love of God in what is being said here?" I had been confronted with an objection to my way of church that, in essence, could be summarized as follows: You can't have personal accountability or a steady diet of biblical input unless you go to an organized church. Otherwise, you're pretty much on your own and at risk of all sorts of spiritual problems.

I began reasoning through it by reminding myself that these relationships I mentioned are very close and involve accountability, and the environment of unconditional love and acceptance gives me and others the freedom to be open and honest. I also thought about how I have plenty of interaction with Scripture and God. In fact, it's even more intense than when I was in organized church. It's no longer just information presented by one person in the form of a sermon, which tends to be one-way communication. Instead, I benefit from multiple perspectives of Scripture, and I interact with others and God by fleshing things out through questions and conversation.

Then I realized, if I choose to accept what this person is telling me, it could just as well lead to detrimental dependencies, like relying on one person's interpretation and teaching for biblical input or the deception that attending groups and meetings is synonymous with accountability. I felt that his underlying premise suggested that somehow I'm less connected to God and my relationship with God is somehow tainted because I'm not doing it his way.

So my freedom filter went to work. I chose not to take this person's opinion on as my own. I left his opinion with him. If he is experiencing accountability and spirituality, as well as receiving the biblical input he feels that he needs at Cedar Creek, more power to him! That's freedom—enjoying the way God is orchestrating "church" for me, without judging others and criticizing their way. So I responded by saying, "God is using the relationships I have and the people I come across in daily life to fuel my desire to know God more intimately and express God to others. For me, this is church. Sounds like your involvement in Cedar Creek is your way of doing church. Cool!"

Many social observers agree that the Western world is experiencing a profound cultural shift, often referred to as a "postmodern" worldview. One feature of this view is that the world has no center: there is no absolute or universal Truth, only differing viewpoints and perspectives. Postmodernism says that Truth is objective and claims the best we can come up with is an imprecise interpretation of the Truth based on bias. Postmodernism also points out that the mediums we depend on for transmitting truth, such as language and scientific observation, are themselves flawed and unreliable.

I can accept this postmodern view as it relates to the little-*t* truth of our world, the physical or sensory dimension of our lives. But I've also discovered that big-*T* Truth belongs to a spiritual realm. It's not a *what* but a *who*. It's God himself. My mind is not capable of conceiving spiritual Truth. However, I'm finding that God has placed a spiritual On-Star system within me to guide me along the paths of spiritual Truth. His Spirit confirms with my spirit what is Truth.

Jesus said his mission was to set captives free (Luke 4:18). I'm finding that when I use freedom as a filter, it's a head-and-gut way of discerning Truth. I can feel deep within my spirit when I am being pulled or enticed into some form of captivity. Upon feeling this, I begin reasoning along the lines of whether or not whatever idea, claim, or action before me will lead to freedom or bondage. With my head and gut working together, I find I am capable of discerning the path of Truth.

Freedom Filter
On? Off?

chapter**eleven**

If I Ever Meet an Angel

Are We Receiving Help from Another World?

There's a stretch of Interstate 65 that runs through north-
ern Indiana into Illinois that can defeat you if you're the
slightest bit weary. I've driven it a few times on road trips
from Nashville to Chicago. This flat piece of highway cuts
through never-ending farmland with a monotony that is
almost unbearable. Once, going to a conference in the north-
west suburbs of Chicago, I tried to do the drive without stopping. I left Nashville in the afternoon in hopes of getting to
Chicago in the wee hours of the morning to avoid traffic,
which could add a couple of hours to your trip if you got
caught in it.

Despite the continual flow of coffee, crossing the Indiana
state line I was whipped. It was about 2:30 a.m. and there
wasn't much traffic on the road. It was just me, Eric Clapton,
and miles and miles and miles of pavement and flatland.

Driving along, I started to doze. I would slowly begin slipping into unconsciousness and then jerk out of it. Each time it scared me a little more and I would tell myself to stay alert and focused. I changed CDs, rolled down my windows, took a big swig of cold coffee, anything to keep me awake. But my dozing spells became more frequent until I was finally out—totally, unequivocally, absolutely dead to the world and behind the wheel.

I have no idea how long I was asleep when suddenly a blaring horn starkly revived me back into consciousness just in time to keep the car from running off the road. After regaining my composure, I looked into my rearview mirror and a huge eighteen-wheeler was following close behind. He saved my life! I was wide awake now and popped in a book on tape I had brought along to listen to. I looked back into my rearview mirror to offer a wave of thanks to the trucker and he was . . . GONE! The truck had vanished into thin air. How can an eighteen-wheeler right behind me completely disappear from the interstate in the five seconds it took me to pop in a tape that was sitting in my front seat?

■ ■ ▓

One day out of the blue I received an e-mail from a guy named Oteil. He read *Divine Nobodies* and wanted to meet. The further along I read, the more interesting it became. This was Oteil Burbridge, bass player for the Allman Brothers Band. He was also in a group named Oteil and the Peacemakers, playing at a downtown music club that Friday night. Oteil invited me to the show so we could meet.

At the club, I hunted down Oteil to introduce myself.

Without hesitation, he threw his arms around me . . . and didn't let go. We talked and laughed together for a few minutes. It was like meeting my long-lost brother despite the fact we had never met before.

The show began, and while watching and listening to Oteil, I was suddenly transported back in time to Mike Smith's basement. Mike Smith was my best friend in high school. His father died at forty-two from a heart attack, and his older brother shot and killed himself several months later. Mike was an exceptional guitar player, and I would listen to him play along to Jimi Hendrix records in his basement.

Mike started drinking alcohol to cope with the pain of his father's and brother's deaths. He dropped out of school, and I was about the only person he allowed into his life. Mike's alcohol problem got worse and most nights he would drink himself unconscious. He soon began taking sleeping pills with his alcohol. Early one morning, the ringing of the phone roused me. Mrs. Smith informed me that Mike had been pronounced dead an hour earlier. He had taken his pills, drank his bottle, and drifted off to an endless sleep. After a long, painful silence, I hung up.

Now watching Oteil, Mike returned to my mind and heart. The physical resemblance between the two is stunning, right down to a small but distinct gap between their front teeth. As I was seeing and hearing Oteil play on stage, it was like I was experiencing Mike in his basement. After all these years, that painful silence lives on in me through Mike's absence. For reasons I don't fully understand, that brief encounter with Oteil brought me peace about Mike's death. During that long and tight embrace with Oteil, I felt I was embracing Mike himself, and Mike was letting me know that he was okay.

Why this experience came twenty-five years after his death, I do not know.

■ ■ ■

I mentioned in a previous chapter meeting Nihad, who introduced to me an Iranian family needing English tutoring. I also met with Nihad from time to time to share the progress we were making and seek her input about developing a relationship with this family and other ways I could help them. In the process I got to know a bit about Nihad and her journey.

Born in Iraq to a devout Muslim family, two unchangeable characteristics about Nihad marked her defenseless under Sadaam Hussein's regime: she was an ethnic Kurd and a woman. War and persecution had steadily dwindled the Kurdish population, while Saddam's Anfal campaign sent Iraqi tanks flattening countless villages and killing thousands. Attending an education institution in Kirkuk, one night after an exhausting day of classes, Nihad went to bed, drifting into the unconsciousness of deep sleep.

The next thing Nihad remembered was standing on a long, stretching desert road leading out of Iraq. How she got on it and where it was going she did not know, but this road was real as real could be. Such is the manner of dreams; while you're in them, they are your only reality. Ahead in the distance on this road she saw three Kurdish men, whom she recognized as classmates. As Nihad watched, one of them pulled an object out of his pocket and tossed it in the sand on the side of the road. Nihad began walking toward the spot where she had seen this and discovered the object flung to the ground was a stunningly beautiful cross.

Taking the cross into her hands, she marveled at its beauty. Spotting a large rock ahead, she decided this was a perfect place and positioned the cross so other would-be travelers would behold its magnificence. Continuing on her journey, she came upon a small village and began searching for someone familiar. Suddenly a dreadful feeling that something terrible had happened to the beautiful cross seized her. Hastening back down the desert road, she was relieved to find the cross undisturbed but discovered something else. Beside the rock something was buried in the sand. Nihad dug up a wooden chest. Brushing it off and opening it, she was speechless in finding the chest filled with exquisite diamonds and priceless pearls. Thrilled and overjoyed with her treasure, Nihad was abruptly awakened from her sleep.

With word of persecution worsening in Kirkuk, Nihad fled for the Iraqi countryside, which soon after became unsafe as threats of violence against Kurds intensified. Plotting her escape, she risked her life and crossed the border into Iran by night on mule. While trekking through treacherous desert mountains, her then–three-year-old dream mysteriously but lucidly surfaced in her mind. Nihad realized she was traveling the long, stretching desert road out of Iraq she had been on in her dream. Bumping along, the meaning of Nihad's dream became clear to her. The desert road leading out of Iraq that she had dreamed of represented the sparing of her life and successful escape from Saddam's persecutions. The beautiful cross was a sign from God that he had given her the dream, that she might know it was he who had spared her life.

Two more dreams were instrumental in stimulating a desire within Nihad to know Christ and guide her to the United States to fulfill a specific mission. She moved to Nashville to start a school for Muslim women, mostly Iraqi and Iranian Kurds. In addition to teaching English, she offers a multitude of life-skills classes aimed at bettering the lives of these women. The name of her school is the School of Dreams and Visions. New students always ask why Nihad gave the school this name. She tells them God speaks to her in dreams, and she reminds the women this is God's way, and they should be open to it. Nihad knows from personal experience that this is one avenue always open for God to guide one to truth and the love of Christ.

■ ■ ■

Did God save my life on Interstate 65 that night with an angel driving an eighteen-wheeler? Was God allowing me to experience Mike's presence through Oteil in that club in order to heal an old wound? Did God guide Nihad through a series of dreams?

It's perplexing how with all my knowledge of the Bible, I managed to miss the numerous examples in Scripture of people who experienced angels, visions, dreams, and mysterious encounters as an integral part of their journey with God. For example, angels in the Bible fulfilled a variety of significant functions, such as conveying information, shielding or protecting, rescuing, and caring for people's needs. In several cases it's a situation where there's more going on than the careless eye can see, so an angel points it out. Angels are seen in Scripture guiding people in the way God wants them to go in a particular situation, sometimes calling them to take a specific action.

The Nicene Creed begins, "We believe in one God, the

Father, the Almighty, maker of heaven and earth, of all that is, seen and unseen." Apparently angels are in that category of the "unseen." The idea of a guardian angel comes from Psalm 34:7, which reads, "The angel of the LORD stays close around those who revere Him, and He takes them out of trouble" (NLV). In Matthew 18, Jesus speaks of children having their own angels: "Watch that you don't treat a single one of these childlike believers arrogantly. You realize, don't you, that their personal angels are constantly in touch with my Father in heaven?" (v. 10 MSG).

In Acts 12:15, the people at John Mark's mother's house thought their servant was seeing Peter's assigned angel at the doorway, when it was really Peter who had just escaped jail, thanks to help from an angel. The verse reads, "'You're out of your mind,' they told her. When she kept insisting that it was Peter, they said, 'It must be *his angel*'" (emphasis added). Whether the jail-breaking angel really was "assigned" to Peter (as they thought) or a different angel assigned just to the task is not said, but he sure looked like Peter.

Thomas Aquinas insisted that God gave everyone their own guardian angels. In their protective roles, angels are in no way depicted in Scripture as Precious Moments–like cream-puff figurines. They can be the fiercest of warriors and the swiftest of rescuers, and angelic determination knows no bounds. After all, they're on a mission. From God! The Bible even instructs us to be prepared to offer hospitality to strangers since, "Some people have entertained angels without knowing it" (Hebrews 13:2).

I also discovered dreams and visions hold special significance in the Christian tradition. In addition to being a common way God spoke to and guided people in the Old Testament,

dreams and visions directed Mary and Joseph in the circumstances surrounding Jesus' birth. After the resurrection and
ascension of Jesus, Peter announced the new era of Christ's
Spirit indwelling believers would result in seeing visions and
dreaming dreams (Acts 2:17).

Digging around in church history, I learned there are nearly
fifteen hundred years of Christians believing visions and dreams
are a natural way that spiritual reality reaches out and touches
people, and a frequent means of God's involvement in our
lives. The major fathers of the early church, both East and
West, from Justin Martyr to Irenaeus, from Clement and
Tertullian to Origen, and Cyprian to Ambrose and Augustine,
believed dreams were a means of revelation.

Before meeting Nihad, I did not give much legitimacy to
dreams, and I even thought people who did were a little loopy.
I was left wondering why I categorically dismissed something that was such an important aspect of people's relationship with God in Scripture and in the lives of Christians down
through history. Sadly, I began seeing my pick-and-choose
approach to the Scriptures. Bible teachings that I could understand and that allowed me to be in control were accepted,
but those beyond human logic, too subjective, or beyond my
control were shelved. For me, dreams and visions were part
of this nebulous, subjective, illogical class of things. Attempting
to understand them was like trying to nail Jell-O to a wall.

Pondering all this, an unsettling thought hit me. What if
all the stuff in the Jell-O category is an important part of
knowing God and experiencing the present reality of his
kingdom? People once thought the world was flat, and the
fear of sailing off the edge of the earth kept them from exploring new territory. Likewise, we have come to believe that

there is only a flat land of consciousness on which to find and experience God, and it is utter folly to go beyond these known horizons. Yet Nihad encountered God through her dreams. People speak of encounters with angels, tell stories of premonitions that saved their lives, and describe situations where a series of highly improbable events occurred, mysteriously leading to an encounter that profoundly impacted them.

Is it possible that coincidence is God's way of getting our attention? Could divine resources surround us, offering help to guide us along the way? Does God sometimes "bend the rules" of our physical reality, enabling us to have certain life-altering spiritual experiences? There are myriad questions left unanswered by our traditional theology.

Walking out of the club that night after meeting Oteil, I felt less fearful of death. In fact, I wanted to explore the subject of death further. Strange, I know. There probably aren't too many folks who eagerly brew a pot of gourmet coffee and find their favorite comfy place to spend an evening contemplating death. I'm beginning to feel this encounter with Oteil was not only meant to mediate the presence of my high school friend Mike for purposes of healing, but also to set the subject of death before me for further exploration. For me, the fear of death, whether it be my own or that of my family and friends, stirs up these despairing feelings of finality and being totally and completely separated from those I love. But what if the physical separation of death doesn't impede a spiritual connection that is real and meaningful? Maybe God allowed me to experience Mike Smith's presence to show me I am not truly separated from him and that I need not fear separation in death.

I remember once as a pastor following a Sunday morning service, someone approached me about a dream they had and asked if I had any inkling as to its significance. Giving it no serious thought, I told the person that God didn't speak through dreams anymore. On another occasion, a woman told me she encountered an angel at the foot of her bed one morning. I alerted the elders to keep their eye on the "angel lady." We human beings are prone to tuning out or thinking impossible any experience that does not fit into some accepted category in our model for the world. I wonder if I did not legitimize these experiences of others because they would have forced me to rethink my belief system or admit there was something I didn't have an answer for.

One of the most surprising discoveries for me these past few years is how many people have stories of remarkable encounters with the spiritual world. I like listening to others tell their experiences because it reinforces to me the truth of God's goodness, love, and intimate involvement in the details of our lives. So often, a person's angel encounter or dream or improbable set of events and encounters result in experiencing God's comfort, healing, guidance, understanding, peace, love, and freedom.

I once experienced a vision that profoundly impacted me. While on a personal spiritual retreat, I discovered an old barn and spent the afternoon there in solitude and reflection. I lit a candle, which I had brought along in my backpack, and placed it on a table in an upstairs room that also had a chair and a little couch. The flickering flame of the candle held my attention as I sat silently. The last thing I remember hearing was a dog barking off in the distance and the fading sound of a pickup truck traveling a gravel road. Suddenly out of nowhere, an image of a dead man walking entered my mind. Wrapped from head to toe in bandages, I distinctly saw a mummy staggering from a coffin's shadow with outstretched arms and stilted legs. Each stumbling step writhed with agony. While seeing this mummy in my mind, I heard a voice say, "Escape the shroud of death and dance!" The coffin's shadow loomed darker, and the mummy's casing grew blindingly brighter as the words slowly languished as fainting echoes in my mind. Then suddenly the picture and the voice vanished.

It felt like hours, but the whole experience only lasted a few fleeting moments. The next thing I remember was the whistling of the wind as it rattled the windowpanes atop the old barn. Never before, nor since, have I had such an experience. It was not a dream, for I was fully conscious. It was not merely a vision, for there was verbal communication I heard in my mind. Having neither been a fan of horror films nor ever claiming to have heard voices, I undeniably knew that this experience was something other than my imagination. Perhaps strangest of all, I immediately understood the meaning of the image and the words.

Starting back in childhood, I began an enslaving habit of fulfilling dysfunctional roles I clung to for self-esteem. In many cases, these roles were a result of my caving in to others' demands and expectations. Like a dog conditioned to roll over in exchange for a treat, I performed the roles in hopes of receiving some bone of self-worth. Some of these roles I identified as "Chameleon"—continually taking the shape of other's expectations; "Star Performer"—striving to accomplish something extraordinary; "Victim"—blaming past wounds as justification for failure; "Healer"—taking responsibility for fixing or compensating for the wounds and sorrows of others. As the story of my life played on, new characters were introduced, fresh backdrops were wheeled in, and different plots emerged, but I stuck to the scripts others handed me. Each time I played the part, another layer of pretense smothered my innermost being and true self to near extinction.

The mummy was a sobering image of how my true identity had been lost beneath a lifetime of artificial roles and functions. The command "Escape the shroud of death and dance!" was God inviting me into new freedom: the freedom to rest in his unconditional love and acceptance and unravel myself from others' demands and expectations in order to be the real Jim Palmer I was uniquely created to be. The vision of the mummy was instrumental, and from time to time God reminds me of it to encourage me to be true to myself.

Sometimes religion too easily wants to pass off or turn a blind eye to people's spiritual experiences. I'm the first to admit that in all my years of professional Christian ministry, I can't ever remember inviting people to share these experiences or organizing groups to explore things such as the significance of dreams, visions, or encounters with angels. Since such an overwhelming number of people purport having such experiences, perhaps it would be helpful if Christendom paid more attention to this and opened these as subjects of study, allowing people to freely tell of these occurrences in their journey with God. Sometimes I wonder if doing so would invigorate a fresh and powerful confidence in God's love and participation in our daily lives.

Fanny Crosby, American hymn writer, is one of the most prolific hymnists in history. She wrote more than nine thousand Protestant Christian hymns during her life, including

"Blessed Assurance," "Jesus Is Tenderly Calling You Home," "Praise Him, Praise Him," and "To God Be the Glory." She was also known for writing poetry from the age of eight. When she was only six weeks old, Fanny developed inflammation of the eyes, which led to her becoming blind. A line in one of her poems reveals that one doesn't need to actually see angels to experience them:

> *Angels descending, bring from above,*
> *Echoes of mercy, whispers of love.*

Maybe one of those angels knows how to drive an eighteen-wheeler.

chapter twelve

Quantum Wonderosity

Has Science Discovered God?

M adeline L'Engle's slight lisp makes you want to listen to her speak. It grabbed my attention just in time to hear her say something that piqued my curiosity. My seven-year-old daughter, Jessica, was listening to a book on CD, *A Wrinkle in Time* by Madeleine L'Engle, who narrates the book herself. I was in the kitchen making a hot dog when Madeline L'Engle began:

> Hello, this is Madeline L'Engle. I'm going to be reading *A Wrinkle in Time* to you. It's a book that almost never got published. I had already had half a dozen books published, but this was a very different one, and nobody knew quite what it was or who it was for. And the general feeling was that it was much too hard for children. Well, my kids were seven, ten,

and twelve while I was writing it and at night I'd read them what I'd written during the day and they'd say, "Oh Mother, go back to the typewriter!" So I knew kids could understand it.

The problem is it's not too difficult for kids; it's too difficult for grownups. Too many grownups tend to put themselves into little rooms with windows that don't open and doors that are locked. And they want to close themselves off from any new ideas.

But you're ready and open for new ideas, and new things, and new places, and new excitements. So I hope you'll enjoy this book. I had a wonderful time writing it.[24]

Madeline L'Engle describes well what it was like during my days of religious Christianity. Looking back, I see my beliefs were the proverbial prison cell of bared windows and locked doors, which my closed mind could not open to experience the comforting, refreshing, and invigorating presence of God. What helped me slide through the bars was approaching God like a child. I realized the bars only kept me from God when I saw myself all grown up, having God all figured out, boxed up, and condensed into some creed or belief system. I could never get to God that way.

God is continually helping me see this through the eyes of Jessica. Jessica isn't very interested in knowing about things theoretically or conceptually; she wants to experience things directly by seeing, smelling, hearing, tasting, and touching them. Her persistent sense of wonder isn't satisfied with others'

24. Madeline L'Engle, *A Wrinkle in Time* (New York: Listening Library, 2006).

findings, but draws her deeper and deeper to knowing and experiencing things herself.

So Jessica asks questions . . . lots of them . . . *lots and lots* of them! Sometimes it drives me batty, well, battier than I already am. Who cares why the sky is blue or why fish have gills or how Peter Pan flies? That's just the way it is!

It seems most folks eventually stop asking so many questions. Apparently, you eventually cross this invisible line where you have more answers than questions. For the most part, people cross that line in their early teens. Any parent can validate the well-known anthropological fact that once a kid turns sixteen, he pretty much thinks he knows everything.

Of course there are exceptions. During my schooling years, I didn't ask many questions because I feared looking stupid. I operated under Mark Twain's axiom: if you think people might suspect you're not so bright, then don't open your mouth and remove all doubt! As an adult, I asked fewer and fewer questions because, frankly, I didn't care. I had enough answers to continue the juggling act of my day-to-day existence. Why should I care about the rest? If scientists wanted to sit around and debate Pluto's planethood, fine. I needed to fill out my NCAA March Madness brackets and root the Braves on to their next World Series Championship.

Questions can also be risky, especially if they have upsetting answers. It's cute for little kids to ask questions—well, most of the time it's cute; sometimes it's downright irritating, but you get my drift. However, for adults, questions can be a very threatening and unsettling part of life. People who ask a lot of questions often find themselves at odds with other people, and even institutions and governments. Sometimes questioning types don't fare very well within religion.

Through his telescope, Italian physicist Galileo discovered the sun was the center of the universe. This contradicted the teaching of the church that the earth was the center, a principle that people in his day believed the Bible taught. In June 1633, the Inquisition found Galileo guilty of heresy on the following grounds: "Namely for having held and believed a doctrine which is false and contrary to the divine and Holy Scripture; that the sun is the center of the world and does not move from east to west, and the earth moves and is not the center of the world, and that one may hold and defend as probable an opinion after it has been declared defined contrary to the Holy Scripture."

Galileo protested, "I do not feel obliged to believe that the same God who has endowed us with senses, reason, and intellect has intended to forgo their use." But it was to no avail; Galileo was condemned to spend the rest of his life locked in his house under guard. He died January 8, 1642. Religion usually assumes its answers are the right answers and doesn't take too kindly to people opening topics for further investigation.

I can certainly relate. After graduating from seminary, I felt I knew all the important God answers. That's why I went to seminary in the first place: to get all my facts straight about God so I could tell others. Yet I reached a point of feeling I pressed as far as I could in knowing God through studying books. Focusing solely on historical narratives, findings, and beliefs tended to perpetuate those same notions in me. It was as if I realized after years of drinking soda pop, I was still thirsty. So I began drinking just plain ol' H_2O. I opened myself to knowing God in whatever and wherever he presented himself.

We've made a lot of progress since the Galileo debacle. Most people now agree that science is a reliable field for determining something like the working model of the universe. But what about science as a means for helping us know more about God?

More than once these last few years, science stepped in and helped reconcile my questions about God. One of my favorite things to do with Jessica is visiting the public library down the street. During one visit, I stumbled across some ideas that helped me put together part of the God puzzle.

In the "new arrivals" section of the library, I found a book about quantum physics and took it back to my seat. The book explains how everything in existence consists of light and heat particles or waves, constantly in motion. These light and heat particles are packets of energy called "quanta," which are the basic elements of all that exists. These energy packets are alive, always moving, interactive, and interrelated to one another.

Sitting in the library, my eyes distinguished everything around me as separate and isolated objects. The laptop resting on the table was a solid object that was separate from me and the table upon which it sat. Turning my head, I saw a tree outside the window separate from the wooden bench beneath it. Off in the distance the cattle were separate from the fields they were grazing in. All of these things appeared distinct and apart from the other.

According to science, this is an illusion. These objects are actually patterns of movement (cow patterns, bench patterns, tree patterns) that change through being in relationship with one another. These changes go beyond the physical nature of the cow hoofs pressing down on the grass or the tree's branches shading the bench; there are nonphysical changes occurring as well. The bottom line is that science tells us that our visible, physical reality has a corresponding invisible, nonphysical dimension (life). Maybe these non-physical interactions are like people telling their flowers how beautiful and full of life they are as a means of encouraging their growth. Material objects appear solid and tangible, yet they are actually composed of organized energy—packets of dynamic light and heat particles.

The quantum physics book went on to say how difficult it is to find language for describing this nonphysical reality and perhaps the best counterpart to "physical" reality might be "spiritual" reality. The word jumped out at me. *Spiritual.* Hmm . . . science discovered some "spiritual" reality beyond words as the all-encompassing essence or root of all existence. When you can detect its energy but your microscope can no longer see it, you run into "spirit." My mind was racing. Quantum physics hadn't *discovered* God, but it was *describing* Spirit. What if the "energy packets" are God? The idea stirred my interest. Oddly, physicists were pointing the way to God!

About that time, Jessica wandered over to my table in the library and asked, "What are you reading, Dad?"

"Oh, this new science book," I replied.

Jessica sat down and began thumbing through some books she'd found—*Pony Pals*, her favorite book series. While rolling around this quantum physics stuff, I started wondering what Jessica might say about it. So I asked, "Jessica, do you ever wonder what God really is?"

"Sure, Dad," she said.

I responded, "What if God is spirit?"

"What is spirit?" she said.

Shooting from the hip I replied, "Spirit is something invisible; it's not a physical thing like this table."

She asked, "What does spirit do?"

"Spirit does everything—like energy, it gives life," I replied.

This was getting fun, as the gears of her curious little mind kept it going with her simple questions. "What is energy or life?" she asked.

I thought for a moment and said, "It's stuff that causes everything to exist."

"Like what?" she asked.

"Well, like the chair you're sitting on, the tree outside that window, the cows out in that field, and of course you too. Like all the stuff you read about in your *Pony Pals* books."

At that, she was satisfied and resumed looking at her own books. But our little discussion multiplied questions in my own mind.

So I decided to keep the conversation going with myself by asking simple Jessica-type questions and responding with simple Jessica-type answers. In case this concerns you, I really don't have many conversations with myself like this. (I do have quite a few conversations with my dog, Jack, and maybe that should concern you . . . and me.) I scribbled out these questions and answers on the front and back of a piece of notebook paper.

I have them laid out below as dialogue. I hope seeing them this way will encourage you to consider listening more intently to your inner child. To make it easier to follow, I identified the two people talking as "Jim," grownup Jim; and "Jamie," the name used for me throughout my childhood. Here goes!

Continuing from where we left off . . .

JAMIE. *So God is in all trees, animals, and humans?*

JIM. *Everything that exists began in God. Because it began in God, it is part of God. Nothing can exist apart from God, because God is what enables everything to exist.*

JAMIE. *Is the tree outside that window God?*

JIM. *The tree is part of God, but not all of God. Just like a branch is part of a tree but not all the tree, or like your hand is part of your body but not all of your body. God isn't a specific part but the sum total of all that exists, the seen and the unseen.*

JAMIE. *So God is e-v-e-r-y-t-h-i-n-g?*

JIM. *Yes! God is all. Maybe this is what Paul meant when he wrote, "For from him and through him and to him are all things." Maybe everything is "from God" because God started it. Everything is "through God" because God is the life energy that enables everything to continue living or being. Everything is "to God" because everything is part of (or has a relationship with) God.*

JAMIE. *What about people, do all people naturally have a "relationship" with God?*

JIM. *All people have a relationship "to" God, but not all people exist in relationship "with" God. It's kinda like everyone in the United States of America has a relationship "to" the president as citizens, but not all citizens have a relationship with the president, like being his friend. The president could never have a relationship "with" all the citizens of the United States of America, because he could never connect and stay connected with all citizens. But God connects with every person all the time, like air, so he is always available to have a relationship with every person who wants one.*

JAMIE. *Does God relate to people differently than he relates to trees and animals?*

JIM. *Yes. Humans have a part of God that trees and animals don't have, and that is self-awareness. Self-awareness means humans know they are alive and living while trees and animals do not know they are alive; they go through the motions of living by instinct.*

When a dog is hungry, it eats; if tired, it sleeps. We can be both hungry and tired and choose not to sleep. In the same way, trees and animals can't choose to have a relationship "with" God. They just go through life in relationship "to" God.

JAMIE. *Why didn't God just make us like trees and birds? What's the big deal about "self-awareness" and "choice"?*

JIM. *God knows that being conscious of and living our spiritual identity is what brings the greatest joy to both God and us. God is already complete within himself; he is God and he knows it. But God is also pleased and fulfilled when you and I come to know who we are. We don't truly "know" until we are aware of it, accepting it, cooperating with it, and expressing it. In other words, walking in the truth of who we are delights God and completes us.*

JAMIE. *Walking in the truth of what? If God is life, energy, or spirit, how do we know God and become an expression of God? It sounds pretty impersonal to me. Be energy? Is God a cosmic battery or something? Does that make me a battery cell?*

JIM. *Well, the highest form of energy is the one that has the greatest impact. The form of energy that has the greatest impact in everyone's life is love, pure and perfect unconditional love. It's no surprise then that 1 John 4:8 says, "God is love."*

JAMIE. *So.*

JIM. *Well, is love impersonal? Can a battery give love or receive love?*

JAMIE. *No.*

JIM. *So God can't just be some impersonal force or energy. He is love, which is personal. What comes to mind when you think of love?*

JAMIE. *When I think of love, I think of times when I have felt love. So love must be some sort of personalized feeling or nature we can experience.*

JIM. *Exactly! Think of a boy's very first Little League baseball game. Let's say the boy strikes out every at-bat and his team loses badly. Now imagine them riding home in the car and his dad announcing they are going to Dairy Queen to celebrate. The boy says, "Celebrate? Celebrate what?! I was a big failure." When they get to Dairy Queen and park the car, Dad turns around to the boy in the back seat. He looks him firmly but tenderly in the eyes and says something the boy never forgets: "Son, I love you. You bring me great pleasure and joy just because of who you are. I love being your father. If you never get a hit this entire season, I'll love you the same as if you hit every pitch out of the park. You are the apple of my eye. There's nothing you could ever do to change that."*

Imagine how the boy feels. The boy sits basking in the warmth of his father's love. It's not a physical warmth like actually feeling the heat of the sun. It's a spiritual warmth like rays of love shining within you.

JAMIE. *So, putting it together, God is . . . well . . . an intimate, loving, caring, life-giving energy or spirit?*

JIM. *Yes, and this intimate, loving, caring, life-giving energy is the root of all living things.*

JAMIE. *So, if trees and animals are rooted in God, does that mean God's love is in them too?*

JIM. *Well, I can tell you this much. I've felt love around trees and dogs. I have hiked wooded trails and felt love. I have held my dog Jack in my arms and felt love. One way or another, the explanation has to be God. Whether it was the love in me or the love in them or both, love can't be experienced without love because God is love.*

JAMIE. *Okay, I remember you saying, "God is e-v-e-r-y-t-h-i-n-g." If God is everything and every-where all at the same time, how can he fit into me? How can you get the ocean into a bottle?*

JIM. *Maybe it's like this. Right now there is a floor lamp turned on next to my table. Though I can't explain it all, there's a connection between the light bulb in that lamp and a power plant sixty miles away. The lamp, the electrical wiring, the high-tension lines, and the power plant itself are all part of a delivery system. The invisible energy produced by the power plant flows through miles and miles of electrical wire* to our house to cause the light bulb in that lamp to glow and illuminate. The energy inside that light bulb, causing it to glow, is just a small portion of the energy produced by the power plant.

Our connection with God is like the power plant's connection with the light bulb, except that God doesn't travel through power lines like electricity does. Since God is e-v-e-r-y-t-h-i-n-g, we are always plugged in. We are actually part of that energy system. Maybe this is what God meant when he said, "Let us make man in our image" or what Jesus meant when he said, "The Father and I are one" and then prayed we would experience that oneness.

JAMIE. So you are saying that you and I are God?

JIM. In a way, yes, and in another way, well, not exactly. The difference between being an expression of God (the light bulb) and the source of God (the power plant) is enormous. The power plant may power my bulb, but if it were to shoot all its power my way it would not only explode my little bulb, it would burn down my house and most of my neighborhood. That power has to be stepped down through a series of transformers in order to be usable at my level. On the way to our house, the power plant's energy goes through transformers, converting the energy into something we can use in our house to toast bread and cook spaghetti.

Similarly, God transforms himself into useful things for our lives, like love, joy, peace, and freedom. So when we express those things as part of who we are, we are expressions of God in the same way that light *from the light bulb is an expression of the energy produced by the power plant. I wonder if the Holy Spirit is our internal God transformer; but maybe God isn't being transformed into something human, rather we humans are being transformed into something like God, expressions of God.*

JAMIE. *Wow, what does that look like?*

JIM. *You already know what it looks like.*

JAMIE. *Huh?*

JIM. *Jesus. Jesus was the perfect expression (light bulb) of God (energy). He demonstrated what it looks like to be fully God, fully human, one person.*

JAMIE. *Yeah, but that was Jesus.*

JIM. *Well, that Jesus said you would do even greater things than he did. We probably aren't consistently expressing even one watt of our gazillion-watt capacity.*

JAMIE. *Does that mean I should be able to walk on water? Maybe leap tall buildings or something like that?*

JIM. *Keep in mind the transforming power or energy God expressed through Jesus was love. God is love. Not just love, but perfect love. The kind of love that is continuously patient, kind, not envious, not boastful, not proud, not rude, not self-seeking, not easily angered, and not keeping record of wrongs. The kind of love that never delights in evil, always rejoices with the truth, always protects, always trusts, always hopes, always perseveres, and never fails. Maybe living that kind of love is the "greater things." And maybe living that kind of love would make walking on water seem like taking out the garbage.*

JAMIE. *Whoa, living that kind of love really would be a miracle!*

JIM. *It's impossible when we are not conscious of being love, loved, and in love ourselves, you know, being plugged into the source of love, God. When we are conscious of our being an expression of God (love), all of that is possible and more. Paul put it this way in Philippians 4:13: "I can do everything through him who give me strength."*

JAMIE. *Why haven't I come to these kinds of understandings before now?*

JIM. *Have you been seeking truth?*

JAMIE. *Sort of.*

JIM. *Sort of?? I mean, have you been seeking God "with all your heart" and his kingdom "first" above all things in life? For me, it all started when I felt secure enough in God's love to push open my windows, unlock my doors, and open for exploring the wide open spaces of God. The more I discovered, the more I wanted to know. I felt like a merchant who had stumbled across a fine pearl and sold everything to buy it and have it as my own.*

JAMIE. *Yeah, well, that's you, Jim. You're some guy who writes books about God. Sometimes I feel like I am so far away from God, God's kingdom, and God's truth.*

JIM. *Aren't we the same? Not just Jim and Jamie, but you, the reader, and everyone else. Aren't we all expressions of the same life, part of the same body? You are never far from God. The times when you feel the farthest from him are the times you are closest to him. Why? Because God's power and life and energy and love is the strongest when you are the weakest. God does not have to move from where he is to where we are; rather, we have to become consciously aware that he is with us in every moment. As Paul said in Acts 17:27–28: "God did this so that men would seek him and perhaps reach out for him and find him, though he is not far away from each of us. For in him, we live and move and have our being. . . . We are his offspring."*

If you're willing to be curious about God like a child, you'll find he is much bigger than what a grown-up mind is capable of conceiving. I've learned not to limit God to "the box" of my current set of beliefs, because there always seems to be something new and more just outside the lines of my present understanding. If you're open to the wonder of God, you won't be disappointed. Michelangelo prayed, "Lord, make me see thy glory in every place."

Seeing God differently is also altering how I view the world around me. For many years I viewed Christianity as a means of escape from my present reality. God and heaven were up in the sky, and eventually I'd be up there, thanks to Jesus. Until then, the goal was to try harder to squeeze as much God as I could into this godless world. As much as I could not imagine taking Jessica to the mall and abandoning her there to fend for herself alone, somehow I thought that's what God had done with his kids—us. Does it make sense that God would abandon his creation?

Sometimes perspective is the key. If something is huge, the closer you are to it, the more imperceptible it is. If I'm out in space I can get a good look at the entirety of the earth, but when I'm walking around on it, it's too massive to discern. There is no vantage point that will give us a complete view or perspective of God, because he is too close for us to know in the way we typically know things. God is so all-encompassing, we can miss him. We essentially come to know God through experiencing him. It's like "knowing" the wind. You can't see it, but you feel it across your face. Once you open your windows and unlock your doors, you know God through experience—his presence, his voice, his love, his peace, his joy.

The apostle Paul explains that our minds have been blinded and we have not been able to see the light. He writes, "For God, who said, 'Let light shine out of darkness,' made his light shine in our hearts to give us the light of the knowledge of the glory of God in the face of Christ" (2 Corinthians 4:6). In other words, God's loving presence at the ground of our being prompts our darkened minds to recognize the truth expressed as Christ. What truth? The same truth science is bumping into—Spirit. An intimate, loving, caring, life-giving energy is the root of all living things and is sustaining all creation and our present reality. We call this "God," whose nature was perfectly expressed as Jesus, who is described in the book of Hebrews as "the radiance of God's glory and the exact representation of his being, sustaining all things" (1:3).

When Jessica was a toddler she had a stuffed bear called Ojo, named after a bear cub from the children's television program *Bear and the Big Blue House*. Everywhere Jessica went Ojo went with her, especially in bed at night. Ojo was a source of great comfort, security, and happiness, and he was always available to be picked up, held, tossed around, and brought along. Ojo did everything he was told. He graciously attended every tea party, agreeably rode right next to Jessica on every car trip, and was okay with lying for long lengths of time smothered beneath a pile of blankets on Jessica's bed until she noticed him missing. Ojo didn't argue when we spilt pancake batter all over him and had to put him in the washer, and he didn't complain about the times he had to spend the night in the freezer because of Jessica's allergy problems. He even got dropped in the toilet once and never said a word. Jessica loved Ojo—but think about it, Ojo was nothing more than fabric, buttons, thread, yarn, and fiberfill.

Then the day came when we went to the animal shelter and adopted our dog, Jack. Jack is completely different than Ojo. Jack has a mind of his own. He gets into things you wish he wouldn't. He'll sneak up on you while you're dead asleep on the couch and lay a big slobbery lick on your face. Sometimes I'll be working on my laptop and this strange feeling of being watched will come over me. I lift my eyes and meet a pair of dog eyes peering at me just over the top of my screen, wanting a little acknowledgment and a wrestling match on the floor. Jack chewed up my favorite baseball hat and a new pair of Pam's shoes. Dan Patrick of ESPN would describe him by saying, "You can't control Jack. You can only hope to contain him."

Since getting Jack, I don't see Ojo around much anymore. Even though Jack is a live wire, the love Jessica and Jack share is so much better than the comfort and safety Ojo supplied. Jack is very protective of her. The other day Jessie said to me, "Dad, Jack loves me and I love him too." You can't always get Jack to do what you want when you want him to, but holding Jack in her arms is infinitely better than dragging Ojo around.

For many years, the God I had fashioned in my mind was a lot like Ojo—safe, predictable, and accommodating. I had so thoroughly equated God with the Bible, it was like I was carrying around God himself, all zipped up inside my leather Bible cover. As I've explored the wide open spaces of God, I've been equally amazed by two discoveries. First, *God is immense, far reaching, and all-encompassing.* Given that God is Spirit, it's near impossible to draw boundaries to contain God. At times religion induces fear in people in response to the enormity of God. It would be right in doing so, if it weren't for the second discovery—*God is perfect love.* There is a peace deep within myself from knowing that all things are held within and sustained by the love of God.

I put away that stuffed God I had all stitched up with my human understandings and fears. God is less formulaic and quantifiable as he once used to be, but experiencing the reality of his love is infinitely better than dragging that other one around. I know exactly what Jessie means: "God loves me and I love him too."

chapter**thirteen**

If Everyone Loved

Where Have All the Little Christs Gone?

> *Where have all the flowers gone?*
> *Long time passing.*
> *Where have all the flowers gone?*
> *Long time ago.*
> —PETE SEEGER

These lyrics written in the early 1960s entered into my world fifty years later via e-mail. The author of the e-mail intentionally altered the lyrics to form a different question, which may end up as one of the most important queries of our day.

Pete Seeger's folk song takes you through a cycle of loss from beginning to end, to beginning again. In the first verse the flowers are gone because little girls picked them all. The little girls grow up, get married, and move on with life and they are gone. Their husbands become soldiers, go off to war, are killed and buried in graveyards, gone once again. Eventually the graveyards disappear, overtaken by flowers. The little girls return picking the flowers, repeating the tragic tale yet again. Finishing as it starts, the song asks, "Where have all the flowers gone?"

The e-mail arrived early one morning from my neighbor friend Judie. Part of getting to know Judie involved sharing our respective spiritual journeys. I shared how discovering God's unconditional love and acceptance in Christ was changing me. We both experienced Jesus as love and peace, and we were encouraged by Jesus identifying these as distinguishing characteristics of his disciples. Judie is someone who holds the highest regard for Jesus Christ and considers him her role model, yet she never dug into the world of religion, nor its accompanying teachings and specifics about the life of Christ. Let's just say her interactions with Christians didn't spark a motivation to engage whatever it was they were focusing on. In one conversation I mentioned that Jesus' first followers lived out his example and teachings with such devotion they became known as "little Christs."

Judie had been mulling over my "little Christs" comment and came to a disturbing conclusion, which she expressed in her e-mail. Jesus' message, displayed in his life, was love and peace. His first followers accepted that reality and lived it. But pondering the present world and her own life experiences, she was left to wonder, "I kept hearing the song 'Where Have All the Flowers Gone?' in my head, except I was hearing it with the words 'little Christs' . . . 'Where have all the little Christs gone?'" It was more than a clever rhetorical question. Even though her personal goal in life is being the same love Jesus is, Judie didn't seem to cross paths with many choosing to live this way, though many people call themselves Christians.

She has a point. Many people choose to fill their world with hate, hurt, division, fear, and despair, even though we are all desperate for love and peace. Statistically, the world is chock-full of "Christians"—intelligent Christians, artistic Christians, successful Christians, church-going Christians, politically active Christians—but what about "little Christ" Christians? Christians who risk everything for love? What about Christians who love indiscriminately, unconditionally, and sacrificially? Apparently, these kinds of Christ-followers are MIA. Every now and then, one like Mother Teresa pops up and we practically create a cult around them because they live an existence so decisively beyond our normal way of living.

I worried a bit that perhaps I talked too much about love in this book. What I'm finding myself is that virtually every aspect of knowing God is related to love. Here are several examples of how love altered my understanding of God and my relationship with him and others.

Before: God is synonymous with religion.
Now: God is synonymous with love.

Before: Christianity is a belief system.
Now: Christianity is a school of love carried out in apprenticeship to Christ.

Before: God hates sin because it disgusts him.
Now: God's motive for hating sin is love. Sin causes hurt and suffering for me and others.

Before: I primarily experience God through religious rituals and acts of obedience.
Now: When I am experiencing love, I am experiencing God.

Before: Christian living is trying harder to be more and
do more.
Now: Christian living is an overflow of God's love in
me.

Before: My source of love is outside myself and I'm
dependent on others to supply it.
Now: My source of love is within me, and while I
enjoy the love of others, I'm not dependent on it
and can freely love others without the expectation
of receiving love in return.

Before: I am created in God's image, which means I
have the capacity to make rational choices and
exercise my free will.
Now: I am created in the image of perfect love, which
means love is the core of my identity and I can
choose love.

Before: The main thing is getting people to adopt my
beliefs about God.
Now: Loving people creates desire within them to
know God.

Before: Somewhere out there is God's purpose for my
life, and I must find it.
Now: At every moment, God's purpose for me is to be
love.

Before: Being "in love" is some temporary euphoric
guy-meets-girl experience.

Now: Being "in love" is walking in the conscious awareness of and being dependent on God's love in me and as me.

Before: Tough love is withholding love from others as a means of disapproval or attempt to bring change.
Now: Tough love is loving others without condition, regardless of the result.[25]

Before: The most powerful force on earth is hate.
Now: The most powerful force on earth is love.

Being in love comes with its own supply of courage and conviction, but people concerned about their reputation need not apply. Love often requires relationships with others, and those "others" might not meet the societal standards of normalcy . . . which can stir up controversy. During my religion days, I essentially classified people into three groups. "Believers" were the in-group of people on the same page with our main beliefs and practices. "Unbelievers" were those we associated with in some way, hoping to convert them. Normally, unbelievers were very similar to me in terms of race, culture, and lifestyle. The third group, "really bad people," is actually a subset of "unbelievers," but we pretended they were in a different group altogether. These people's beliefs or behaviors seemed to epitomize everything we were against or didn't believe in. The group was mostly comprised of people

---

25. That's not to say tough love will always subject itself to the continual abuse and victimization of another. That could be enabling a destructive mentality in another that is also ruinous to the abuser.

with erroneous theology and/or politics, or grossly immoral behavior. It was not appropriate for believers to hang out with "really bad people." This is where the religious version of "tough love" kicked in—withholding love altogether.

Now I see these limitations I placed on love had no basis in the life or teachings of Jesus. Jesus pretty much undid my comfortable theory of love when he said, "Love your enemies" (Matthew 5:44). This is a reminder that love is the foundation and, as such, a prerequisite for peace. The religious establishment condemned Jesus for hanging out with "sinners." They had limits on their love; Jesus didn't.

For many years, following Jesus' example of love was implausible because my religious logic pitted my belief in God's "holiness" in conflict with God's "love." At times it made God seem schizophrenic. One minute God was too holy to look upon sinners; the next minute he was hobnobbing with the worst of them. The Christian belief system I constructed rested on the notion that God rejects sinners. Yet Jesus offered unconditional love and acceptance to them (us). Religion often implies one must "clean up your act" before receiving anything from God. Jesus, however, had no qualms about leaving open forever the floodgates of God's favor for people regardless of what condition they were in. Once, when questioned about it, Jesus responded, "It's not the healthy who need a doctor, but the sick" (Mark 2:17). In fact, I think Jesus never had floodgates to begin with. In him, love flowed continuously and without even a means of restraint.

There was a time when I considered Jesus' emphasis on things like love and peace as a nice but unrealistic ideal. My religious sensibilities told me to grow up and let go of those silly, childlike notions. Instead, I acquired a militant view of life. I was a Luke Skywalker–type Christian soldier in a war, striving to defeat Darth Vader and the evil empire. You were either with us or against us. One way or another, it was all headed toward Armageddon.

I began to change the day I became conscious of and allowed myself to receive and depend on the love and peace of God within me. At the center of my being, I experienced the fulfillment of Jesus' words, "All things are possible with God" (Matthew 19:26). Having grown up in a love-starved home, I set out into adulthood striving and groping for love any way I could get it. I turned to Christianity in hopes of fulfilling my need in God. Instead, I began chasing the proverbial oh-so-close-but-just-beyond-my-grasp greased pig of works-based love and acceptance. After reaching top status in the world of Christendom, I felt more empty and weary inside than when I began.

The magnitude of my ceasing to strive, and instead learning to rest in God's love and peace, could be compared to the Cubs winning back-to-back World Series and science figuring out how to produce a fat-free Krispy Kreme donut. There may be no greater miracle than a contented Jim Palmer!

As miracles began happening in my life, I started believing in them. Things I once considered impossible now seemed possible with God. A new kind of logic began forming within me, and I began wondering: *If I can experience peace and love, why can't everyone else? If love and peace are true of my inner world, why can't they exist in my outer world? If I'm not conflicted within myself, why must there be conflict in my relationships with others? Anything is possible.*

God allowed me to soak up and revel in his love and peace for quite a while before letting go of the next shoe, which was God shrinking the distance between my interior experiences and exterior actions. There was no such separation in Jesus of Nazareth. He was love not only because he was perfect love within himself but also because he was an expression of love in the world. Jesus was the Prince of Peace not only because he was perfect peace within himself but also because he was an instrument of peace in the world. Even when violence could have provided some sort of human advantage, Christ told Peter to put away his sword (John 18:11). Jesus' way of establishing his kingdom on earth wasn't going to be through violence and coercion, which Jesus further explained later by saying his kingdom was "not of this world" (John 18:36).

Woven throughout the Bible is a message that will change the world if we accept it: Christ is "the way," and the Christ-way unveils a different way to live. Man's way of division, conflict, strife, schism, greed, egotism, hatred, and war falls away as the Christ-way becomes our new manner of living. It's not just trying harder to add certain characteristics like compassion and self-sacrifice to your life. The key to Jesus' way of life was dependency on the Father. Jesus explained that he only said and did what he saw his Father saying and doing (John 8:28). In other words, the Christ-way is an abiding way. Paul identifies the spiritual qualities of love, joy, peace, patience, kindness, goodness, faithfulness, gentleness, and self-control as the "fruit of the Spirit" (Galatians 5:22–23). The sap within a tree supplies the nutrients, which naturally produce fruit. Likewise, as we abide in God's life of love and peace within us, it naturally produces acts of love and peace in the world.

Jesus demonstrated this kind of abiding life with every breath. Since Christianity is based on Jesus' life, it's reasonable to expect Christianity would help people discover and live in this abiding way in which love and peace are expressed through their lives. Life is complex and sometimes comes at you hard, and conversations about what it means to be an instrument of love and peace in this or that case are necessary. What does it mean if our Christianity isn't motivating these kinds of discussions?

Christianity seems to be in a much different and precarious situation in our day and time compared to its beginnings. Two thousand years ago, the first "little Christs" revolutionized a predominately religious world with the eternal spiritual message of God's unconditional love and peace. Now we seem to live in a world where the Christian message has lost its edge, dulled by the hammer of man imposing conditions and rules to the unconditional nature of God's love. It seems we're back to where we were, before Jesus ever appeared, living in a world of religion instead of living spiritually. Have people heard the "gospel" repeatedly and become weary of it—you know, weary of unconditional love and peace? Or has the gospel been replaced by a Christianity devoid of true love, joy, and peace, and now focused on preserving outworn structures, traditions, and the status quo?

Judie's e-mail question may supply the explanation. Too often the conduct of some Christians has belied and contradicted the message of Christianity. The gospel of love and peace is no longer convincing on the lips of these Christians because they have ceased to be a living example. So the natural question is, "Where have all the little Christs gone?" In the vacuum of their absence, many people turn to some forms of spirituality offering escape from earthly concerns altogether, while complacent Christians eagerly await heaven so the mess of the world can be left behind. Jesus prayed for his kingdom to come "on earth." Maybe we just didn't think he was serious. He was!

God's way of saving the world has always been an inside job. He slips in under the cover of night and beneath the radar and pulls off thirty-something years of living as a nobody carpenter in nowheresville before they kill him. His death only serves to multiply his life exponentially. Now there's not just one Christ in the world; they're everywhere.

Virtually every significant thing God has ever done to birth his kingdom has been contrary to human logic and has come through the least likely people. If you don't believe me, read the Bible. The most convincing evidence that a new world of perfect love will come as a chain reaction begun by a waitress at Waffle House is large numbers of people insisting it's not possible. One little Christ at a time will bring the evolution of reality, and the kingdom of God will be on earth as it is in heaven.

It was a startling revelation for me to discover that "becoming like Christ" was not adding an increasing number of religious activities to my life, but being guided and governed by a totally different way of living and interacting with others in the world.

The "lordship of Christ" became a practical daily choice— my way or the abiding way. Awakening to and resting in God's love and peace within myself supplied what was necessary to be love and peace in the world. However, I've learned that whether resting in God's love and peace within myself or living from that place in the world, the potential for conflict remains. First, as a conflict between man's way and the abiding way within myself. And second, as I am living the abiding way, the conflict it creates with man's way in the world. It would be easy to walk in love and peace if everyone was doing it. But they're not!

Many people have a lot vested in keeping man's way going. The abiding way means relinquishing control, which seems scary and unpredictable if you are not convinced or have faith that God's abundant life is the ultimate reality. That's why a life of love and peace is not some humanly safe, comfortable, serene, or continuous state of euphoric bliss, but the riskiest, most dangerous path of all. There's a reason that everyone's not doing it. Just look at Jesus—he was rejected, ridiculed, hated, abandoned, and killed. Yet Jesus knew death was not a deterrent to his way succeeding.

Even setting aside all the spiritual implications of Jesus' death and resurrection, whenever a person lays down his or her life or pays a significant personal price for living the truth, it only serves to magnify the truth more convincingly. I've learned from personal experience that believing Jesus' message in theory makes you a good Christian, but fleshing out and living the implications of his message can get you in a lot of trouble.

Love is the most transformational force on earth, but judging and condemning is so much easier. There's a lot of resistance to love and peace in the world, even from Christians. If you don't believe me, start hanging out with people in that "really bad" group, and criticism from the Christians will find you. I'd like to hope people act in judgment and condemnation simply because they are unaware of the spiritual principles of the abiding way. For instance, man's way is to point a finger, express disapproval, and manipulate change through fear and shame or refuse to associate with people of questionable behavior. Man's way sometimes affects temporary change but ultimately lacks transformational power, because condemnation never liberates.

The abiding way recognizes that the moral evil of our world results from our alienation from the deepest truth and the springs of spiritual life within us, and our estrangement from God. Paul writes in Titus 2:11–12, "The grace of God that brings salvation has appeared to all men. It (the grace of God) teaches us to say 'No' to ungodliness and worldly passions, and to live self-controlled, upright and godly lives in this present age." So what transforms a person to no longer live according to worldly passions of greed, lust, pride, and hate? According to Paul, the answer is "the grace of God"— the unconditional love and acceptance of God.

How people change is a paradox. Human logic says if we love and accept people unconditionally, it will encourage them to continue destructive behaviors. According to Paul, it's actually what enables or empowers them to say no to these behaviors. Withholding unconditional love from others deprives people access to the only power, the only force, the only reality, the only possibility that can transform their lives and the central truth that gives meaning to all of existence. When I am consciously aware of and dependent upon God's unconditional love and acceptance of me, it is much easier for me to extend this love and acceptance to others. This is another principle of the abiding way: you can't bear love if you yourself are not abiding in love. Love isn't something you create; it's something that overflows from you when you plug into it.

Even as overflow, it's not always a human bed of roses. True love has a certain grit and staying power to it. Despite his disciples being stubborn and slow to learn, Jesus patiently stuck with them to the very end. People of his ethnic and religious roots rejected him, his closest friends betrayed him, but Jesus continued choosing love. His last words to humanity before his death, spoken after they nailed him to a cross of their making were words of love: "Father, forgive them, for they do not know what they are doing" (Luke 23:34). Many of the first Christians met the same fate as a result of living the abiding way and died as martyrs.

The closest some people get to abiding in Jesus' way of love and peace is protesting what they are against. But that begs the question, is there an alternative? And if so, what does it look like? For instance, I think being "pro-peace" is more hopeful than simply being "antiwar." It's hypocritical for me to sit around judging and criticizing soldiers going off to war and the political leaders involved in deploying them, when I'm contributing to the system that helped set in motion the process resulting in that course of action.

As I journey forward with God, I not only become more conscious of his kingdom within me, but I am also more conscious of how I sometimes still choose to live man's way. Here is how I sometimes still choose man's way and what love motivates me to do instead:

1. I unconsciously pass on to others the pain, cruelty, depression, and despair inflicted upon me in my past. Abiding in love heals and transforms my own life, and being healed and transformed perpetuates that reality into the larger world through me.

2. I make my financial independence, my political persuasions, my spiritual preferences and practices, my American identity, or the gratification of my

current desire the highest value. Abiding in love motivates me to recognize God and his kingdom as the highest value, the sap of life. As I live the abiding way, I view each part of my life (personal finances, day-to-day interactions with others, responsibilities of citizenship) as an evolving part of a larger totality where ultimate worth is measured by how close something brings me and others to God, and love of each other.

3. I become overly zealous about my spiritual discoveries, experiences, and place on the journey and suggest them as *the* way or superior to others' spiritual discoveries, experiences, and progress. Abiding in love honors the image of God in everyone and respects all religious traditions and spiritualities seeking God's love for all people. Abiding in love motivates me to walk in spiritual humility, realizing I bring my own limitations to every encounter with God. Yet I enthusiastically share and advocate what I have found compelling in my own relationship with God and encourage others to explore what helps me.

4. I condemn and write off people who commit acts of violence and oppression in the world without aiding in their transformation. Abiding in love motivates me to bring rescue and healing to people who are victimized by the abuse, violence, and oppression committed against them. This same love also seeks the transformation of the abusers, who have often been victims of abuse themselves. Love motivates me

to show more love and care to everyone around me, to take time to know others more deeply, and to perpetuate a world that provides everyone with human dignity and spiritual nourishment.

5. I complacently accept a world with an unjust distribution of basic necessities such as food, water, shelter, livelihood, education, and health care. Abiding in love motivates me to share what I have (money, food, lodging, possessions, transportation, skills) with people in need around me, and it promotes generosity and support toward those who lack throughout the world.

6. I speak words of pessimism, hate, negativity, judgment, gossip, or fear. Abiding in love motivates me to speak words of hope, encouragement, compassion, affirmation, and caring.

7. I consume the world's resources, seeking my own success without consideration of its effect on others. Abiding in love keeps in check my own consumption of the world's resources and promotes ecological sustainability and material modesty. Abiding in love allows me to see the success of others as an inspiration rather than a threat. Being content in the spiritual resources God provides enables me to live life less driven by consumerism and consumption.

The biblical explanation for the abiding way is much more than simply protesting what we see wrong in the world. Paul writes in the book of Romans, "Do not repay anyone evil for evil" and "as far as it depends on you, live at peace with everyone" (12:17–18). A few verses after these remarks, Paul continues with, "Let no debt remain outstanding, except the continuing debt to love one another, for he who loves his fellowman has fulfilled the law" (13:8). It's one thing to feel love and peace within you; it's another thing to be these in the world. Abiding in love breeds confidence in Christians to express love in actions. The spiritual resources within us can sustain us through defending the Christ-way with sacrifices and accepting misunderstanding, injustice, slander, and even imprisonment and death. In 2 Peter 1:3, Peter writes, "His divine power has given us everything we need for life and godliness."

The suffering and strife of the world seems so over-whelming, it's no wonder we dream of escaping and leaving the rest behind. Jesus' desire that God's kingdom exist "on earth as it is in heaven" seems like a pipe dream. However, I'm reminded of the somewhat bizarre adage, "How do you eat an elephant? One bite at a time." How do you end human suffering? One little Christ at a time. Martin Luther King Jr. was one little Christ. Mother Teresa was one little Christ. Asked how she stayed motivated amid such massive and desperate need, Mother Teresa replied, "I never look at the masses as my responsibility. I look only at the individual. I can love only one person at a time. I can feed only one person at a time. Just one, one, one." Too often we idolize the messengers and quote their sayings but miss the essential message of their lives: living the truth at whatever cost. As we live the truth, our lives build a convincing case that there is in fact an alternative way, and that abiding in love is the only way.

Since the writing of *Divine Nobodies*, I have come in contact with all kinds of people who are living the abiding way. As apprentices to Christ, they have allowed him to shrink the distance between their intentions and actions, their words and deeds. They know the world will be transformed as their abiding in God's perfect love and peace overflows into their everyday lives. My guess is they were always there, but I was too blind to notice them as they delivered packages, cut my hair, rang me up at the cash register, and left comments on my blog.

Once you wipe away all the religious labels, there are only two kinds of people in this world: those who are awake and those who are asleep. Some of us are awake to the abiding way Jesus taught, and the rest are still sleeping in their own way. As more people awaken to, abide in, and live the truth, the kingdom of God will become the one and only reality. There's a tipping point when the light of God's kingdom will drive out the shadows of its absence, and the acceleration of a new reality governed by perfect love will be born.

These past few years have deepened within me the conviction that love is the sole force capable of changing me and others. There are all sorts of ways we can manage a "good Christian" image and behave well, but only love has truly transformed my being. As I said earlier, if God is the ultimate power, then he must be love, perfect love. Love would not create an opposing force or power stronger than itself. Even the depths of hate displayed in the horrific tragedy of 9/11 is no match for the power of love. Hate may strike first, but love always trumps hate. If God is love and I am his creation, then I am love. If I am love, then I must only do what love would do. Be love.

If everyone loved perfectly, what would change in the world? What would cease to exist because it wouldn't be needed? A while back a friend and I were kicking this around. Here's what we came up with:

- We wouldn't need governments; if love governed, why would man need to?
- We wouldn't need borders and dividing lines; we wouldn't need to separate ourselves from anyone because we would be at peace with one another.
- We wouldn't need the military; we would no longer wage war or have enemies.
- We wouldn't need police; we would all be protecting and serving one another.
- We wouldn't need money; everyone would give to whoever was in need.
- We wouldn't need hospitals, mental institutions, and doctors. Research shows that disease is often linked to a deficit of love and its effects, and the cumulative negative effect of stress, anxiety, bitterness, and depression is the opposite of perfect love.
- We wouldn't need nursing homes; we would take the elderly into our homes and care for them.

Every system of control instituted by man since the beginning of time wouldn't be necessary. Everyone's behavior and attitudes would be governed by love. Like Paul said, "Christ's love compels us" (2 Corinthians 5:14). The logic of this is growing in me. Does perfect love exist in the kingdom of God? Yes. Is there any hate, division, or suffering in the kingdom of God? No. Where is the kingdom of God? Jesus said, "Within you" (Luke 17:21). It only makes sense that as more and more people are guided by the realities of God's kingdom, the qualities of that kingdom will shape and change our world . . . the snowball becomes an avalanche.

I had to do some convincing with my publisher to get my list of things describing a world where everyone loves perfectly into this chapter. The feeling is that it was too "unrealistic." Admittedly, as I contemplated the list myself, it felt like a huge leap from our present reality. And I am not saying all emotional and physical disease is simply the result of bad choices or some spiritual problem. But maybe the first step forward needs to be setting our sights upon and orienting our conversations around what God's kingdom looks like "on earth as it is in heaven." If we can't even imagine it, can we ever expect to live it? For example, what if there wasn't just one Mother Teresa who lived her life and died, but one hundred thousand of them spread around the world and living that mentality of loving and serving others one person at a time? Or what about one hundred thousand Bonos who are convinced that human tragedies such as HIV/AIDS and poverty can be overcome by people who act in compassion and love?

Where have all the little Christs gone?

Apparently, very few people are capable of envisioning a redeemed world except rock stars.

If everyone cared and nobody cried
If everyone loved and nobody lied
If everyone shared and swallowed their pride
Then we'd see the day when nobody died
—Nickelback

The Love I Found

I crossed the forty-year-old line not too long ago. People normally make a big deal for one's fortieth birthday. The "over the hill" theme is popular, where everyone wears black and someone comes dressed as the Grim Reaper. The irony of it is, I feel more alive now than I ever have. Somewhere along the journey of these past few years, I descended south of my head and began living from my heart. As I experience the world and encounter others, I am acutely aware of certain feelings these experiences and encounters produce inside. The distance between experiencing these feelings within me and expressing them through new ways of thinking, words, and actions is shrinking.

Connecting with the world through your heart makes you vulnerable. It doesn't always feel good, like that unbearable sadness that aches inside me when I catch the woman crying on her front steps as I jog by. But then there are also those moments that remind you how thankful you are that you're not playing dead. Sometimes my family will be sitting together eating dinner and I will look over at Jessie, and suddenly the most powerful feelings of love in all the world will wash over me.

I realize now this is more than simply me living from my heart. I was feeling the sadness of God for that woman as I jogged by, and God's love for Jessica as I looked upon her. I had always known that the Bible says, "For God so loved the world" (John 3:16), but it seems so more real now as I experience God loving the world as me. When I'm paying attention, I find I never come across a person whom God doesn't prompt me to love.

During the Christmas holiday, our family watched *The Muppet Christmas Carol* . . . three times. I watched it a fourth time by myself (I didn't tell anyone). The movie, based on Charles Dickens's book *A Christmas Carol*, connected with Truth deep within me. How tragic that Ebenezer Scrooge had lived so much of his life closed to love, and he hurt others as a result. He had managed his earthly affairs so efficiently, but he was filled with emptiness, loneliness, bitterness, and despair. I could relate. For many years when it came to God, I was knowledgeable, disciplined, busy, and obedient, but I was weary, empty, and weighed down inside.

Ebenezer's heart was so hardened that the only chance of

getting through to him was during his sleep in a dream. It worked! He dozed off that night as a calloused, angry, selfish, and hateful man. He woke up overflowing with a new excitement for life and boundless compassion for all. He was alive to love in every way, expressing it freely and lavishly, and receiving and enjoying the love of others for him. I know in my heart this story of transformation is true. There is no human being beyond the reach and power of God's love, and God has a full arsenal of ways he is willing to express his love, even some downright bizarre ways if necessary. In *The Muppet Christmas Carol*, the narrator says, "The thing that made Scrooge happiest of all was that his life lay before him and it could be changed."

Jessica and I joined with Scrooge and all his beloved friends at their Christmas dinner feast as they sang, "The love we found, the love we found—we carry with us, so we're never quite alone. The love we found, the love we found—the sweetest dream that we have ever known."

Singing along, my heart and spirit felt gloriously free. For I have found this Love, and he is the greatest God I have ever known.

Have patience with everything unresolved in your heart
and try to love the questions themselves.
Live the questions now.
Perhaps then, someday in the future,
you will gradually, without even noticing it,
live your way into the answer.

—Rainer Maria Rilke

Acknowledgments

The birthing of this book was a labor of love, made possible through the encouragement and support of several people. I'm so thankful I live with my best friend, Pam. In many respects, these chapters are the outcome of countless conversations she and I have had about knowing God. Sometimes she's pushing me, and other times I'm pulling her into those wide open spaces; but knowing we journey together brings me joy and peace.

I'm convinced I have the best agent in the world, Greg Daniel. More than once I sent him my manuscript, and after reading it, his response was, "This can be better." Admittedly, at first I contemplated how to stage the perfect murder. We sometimes meet at a nearby Chinese restaurant, and I could have tried sneaking cyanide into his moo goo gai pan. Instead, I realized Greg kept pushing me until I had done my very best. I may have stopped before that point if it hadn't been for Greg.

Of course even after I did *my* best, it still required others to edit content, create a book cover, and get the word out about *Wide Open Spaces*. These are the awesome folks at Thomas Nelson Publishers, whom I appreciate more than they can ever know. Adria Haley and Jennifer Stair improved the book significantly through the editing process.

From start to finish, Rick Harris, Judie Cotrell, and Anne Goodrich appeared at just the right times to offer what I needed to keep pressing forward. Sometimes that was their unconditional love and acceptance; other times it was a kick in the butt. Along with Pam and Greg, Rick and Judie read and reflected upon each chapter and offered invaluable feedback and insight. However, I intentionally did not let them read two chapters so they would have some reason for wanting to read the finished book. Of course they told me they would have read it anyway.

I would be amiss not to mention all my MySpace friends and those who have contacted me at divinenobodies.com. I have grown and learned much from my interactions with these friends, and they have supplied a steady stream of encouragement and insight.

About the Author

Jim Palmer received his masters of divinity degree from Trinity Evangelical Divinity School in Chicago. His background includes pastoral ministry, inner-city service, and international human rights work. Jim Palmer founded and currently leads the Pilgrimage Project, an initiative encouraging the freedom to imagine, dialogue, live, and express new possibilities for being an authentic Christian. As a writer, speaker, blogger, and friend, Jim encourages others who seek to know God beyond the boundaries of conventional religion. Jim enjoys hiking, sketching, conversation, pizza, and life with wife, Pam, daughter, Jessica, and dog, Jack. Jim hosts a weekly podcast show on wiredparish.com and can be reached at divinenobodies.com.